DROPOUTS
A Challenge to Distance Education

DROPOUTS
A Challenge to Distance Education

V P Matheswaran

AUTHORSPRESS

Worldwide Circulation through Authorspress Global Network
First Published 2010
by
Authorspress
E-35/103, Jawahar Park
Laxmi Nagar, Delhi-110 092
e-mail: authorspress@yahoo.com

Dropouts: A Challenge to Distance Education

ISBN 978-81-7273-525-8

Printed in India at Tarun Offset, Delhi.

Foreword

Countries around the world are recognising higher education as a key driver of growth and as a result the demand for higher education increased considerably during the last three decades. But still, the higher education scenario in India is yet to register a growth compared to developed countries. The gross enrolment ration (GER) in higher educational institutions in India is just 12.4 per cent at present whereas the corresponding global average being 23 per cent and it is as high as 50-70 per cent in developed countries. To meet the increasing demand for higher education, Central Government is planning to expand the higher education by establishing more Central Universities and IIMs and the Hon'ble Minister for HRD is very optimistic about increasing the GER to at least 30-35 per cent by the end of this plan period. It may be possible to attain the proposed GER only with a massive expansion of distance education.

The limitations of formal education and the changing needs of higher education aspirants (people who would like to enhance their qualifications while at home or at job) are the reasons for the emergence of correspondence courses, now popularly known as 'distance education'. Though the enrolment in distance education has been increasing since its introduction during seventies and as on date it contributes for more than one fifth of the enrolment in higher education, a close look at the completion rate reveals that the attrition is also high in almost all the distance education institutes or open universities. To achieve higher GER, it is not necessary to expand the distance education but also necessary to ensure that the dropouts rate is kept at minimal. Though there have been a few studies on the school education and formal higher education dropouts in India and abroad, studies on distance education dropouts is scanty in spite of the fact that the 'distance education' as such has been now recognised as a separate discipline. In this connection it is pertinent to note that the National Knowledge Commission (NKC), a high level advisory body to the Prime Minister of India, among other things, rightly recognised the need for a radical reform of the system of Open and Distance Education (ODE) to achieve the objectives of expansion, inclusion and excellence in higher education. Distance education is the only system through which higher education can be provided to all those who desire to pursue higher degree/ diplomas without any socio-economic barriers. But the major problem associated with the distance education, namely, dropouts, has not been properly addressed so far and as a result there is large wastage for the Institute/University as well as to the learners. It is high time that the University administration offering distance education programs take necessary steps to face the challenge of large dropouts and take remedial measures.

As the Vice-Chancellor of an Open University, I deeply appreciate the sincere efforts of Dr.Matheswaran for bringing out this book "Dropouts: A Challenge to Distance Education". I am confident that this book will be very useful to researchers in this field as well as to the administrators of distance education institutes/open universities to understand the problems of distance learners, their expectations and the need to facilitate for successful completion.

In the present hyper competitive global environment organisations including distance education institutes/open universities must constantly invent, evolve and refine their products or services, if they are to remain competitive and profitable and avoid being outpaced by more innovate competitors. In short the maxim here for distance education institutes / open universities today is 'innovate or perish'. In this context, the work of the Dr. Matheswaran gains importance. The administrators of the distance education institutes/open universities need to look into various causes of dropouts in distance education and plug the possible deficiencies so as to remain in the competitive field of providing quality distance education.

Dr. Kalyani Anbuchelvan M.A., M.Phil,Phd.
Vice-Chancellor
Directorate of Technical Education Campus
Guindy, Chennai-600 025.
Tel:+91 44 22351414 Fax:+91-44 22201199

Preface

The real wealth of a nation is its people and as such the economic development of the country depends more on the human development than on any other resources. Education plays a vital role in the formation of human capabilities as real education imparts knowledge, skills, and attitudes. In fine, education is essential for the greater realisation of human potential necessary for the welfare of the individual and the country as a whole.

The tertiary education or higher education is considered as a 'dominant force' in the formation of human development as it is expected to provide more skills and enhance the competencies of human resources. The realisation of the benefits of higher education has increased the demand for higher education considerably. The education system has been changing with change of civilisation and also due to increasing demand. The education system moved on from *'gurukula'* system to 'class room' (formal education) system and then to 'distance education'.

The National Policy on Education (NPE) 1968 suggested further expansion of higher education through 'private study' and 'evening colleges'. But the attempt to popularise the 'private study' did not evoke good response as it entirely depended on the individual initiative without any institutional support.

The 1968 NPE was reviewed in the year 1986 wherein emphasis was given for the consolidation of existing institutions and launching of open learning system to augment opportunities for higher education and also to operate as an instrument for democratising education. Further the NPE 1986 rightly observed that 'the future thrust will be in the direction of open and distance education' as it augments opportunities for higher education to all, ensures cost effectiveness and promotes a relevant, flexible and innovative system of education.

The distance education is basically a form of self study but with various student services from the Distance Education Institution/University. It has become popular worldwide including India across many subject areas and at various educational levels in view of its access without restrictions of time and place and for providing opportunities for higher education to all those who are desirous of pursuing degree / diploma of their choice while continuing their full-time employment.

While studies have been done on various aspects of distance education like, relevance, success, cost, use of multimedia etc. studies on the dropouts are very limited. Fairly large numbers of distance education students encounter difficulties of different nature like, personal and most importantly inaccessibility of assistance of University administration for their varied study related problems and as a result they are forced to discontinue their studies which they joined with so much of ambition. Studies on this vital area are necessary to understand the reality and to make necessary modifications in the delivery system.

As the author has already done some work on distance education including his doctoral level research, the above scenario of distance education kindled him to take up a study on distance education dropouts.

The University Grants Commission (UGC), New Delhi approved the research proposal and funded the project. I wish to record my deep sense gratitude to UGC for giving me an opportunity to undertake a major research project on dropouts in distance education.

I deeply appreciate the cooperation extended by my colleagues in the department for the successful completion of the UGC project as well as in the publication of this book which is an updated version of the Project Report submitted to the UGC. I am thankful to administrative staff members of the department as well as staff members of University administration connected with the research project section for their assistance and cooperation.

I am grateful to Thiru P. V. Ramalinggam, Public Relations Officer, University of Madras for his continued support and encouragement in all my endeavours. I am thankful to Dr.D Venkataraman, Head of the department of Geography Education, Institute of Advanced Studies in Education, Chennai, Mr. Aref Mohamed AM and Mrs.R. Daphne, Research Scholars for their assistance. I wish to thank (Mrs.) Syndia Carolin Rajakumari and Mr.R. Kalanithi, who have worked under this project and executed the laborious task of data collection, compilation, etc.

I am deeply indebted to my beloved parents for their blessings. I wish to thank my wife Dr.A. Parameswari, Department of Chemistry, Presidency College, Chennai and my beloved daughter M. Kural Vani for evincing keen interest in all my academic work.

I wish to thank the management of Authorpress, New Delhi for coming forward to publish this book in a short time without compromising on quality.

V.P. Matheswaran

Abbreviations

AIOU	Allamma Iqbal Open University
APOU	Andhra Pradesh Open University
AU	Athabasca University
CABE	Central Advisory Board of Education
CCTU	Central China Television University
CDE	Centre for Distance Education
COES	College of External Studies
COL	Commonwealth of Learning
DDE	Directorate of Distance Education
DEC	Distance Education Council
DE	Distance Education
DL	Distance Learning
HRD	Human Recourse Development
ICE	Institute of Correspondence Education
ICDE	International Council for Distance Education
IDE	Institute of Distance Education
IGNOU	Indira Gandhi National Open University
NAAC	National Assessment and Accreditation Council
NCERT	National Council for Education, Research and Training

NKC	National Knowledge Commission
ODL	Open/Distance Learning
OL	Open Learning
PCP	Personal Contact Programme
SLOU	Sri Lanka Open University
STOU	Sukkothai Thammathirat Open University
TNOU	Tamil Nadu Open University
UGC	University Grants Commission
UKOU	United Kingdom Open University
UNISA	University of South Africa

Contents

1

Distance Education

India is a home for 17 per cent of the world's total population comprising one billion people with different socio-economic and cultural backgrounds. The formal system of higher education was accessible only to a fraction of the total population. The programmes of study offered by various universities/colleges helped to fulfil limited requirements of particular regions and segments of the society and therefore people had to approach different universities/colleges offering courses of their choice.

Weaker sections of the society find it difficult to receive education of their choice in nearby institutions at affordable costs. The National Policy on Education (1986) recognised that educational opportunity in India is both inadequate and unequal. It emphasised that a cost-effective alternative to the conventional system of higher education can be seen in distance education and open universities, to those who have been deprived of it due to one reason or another.

The modular structure and flexible delivery system makes distance education programme ideal to meet the desired higher educational needs of a wider class of learners.

Evolution of education passed through three stages as follows: The first one is *Gurukula* system, the second is classroom system and the third is distance/open learning system. The *Gurukula* system is where the disciple learns from his *Guru* by living and working in close association with him. The classroom system is the second stage in the evolution of education. With the entry of technology into the world of instruction, the communication revolution resulted in transformation of the education system, resulting in the emergence of distance education.

Distance education is neither a supplement nor a complement to the conventional face-to-face system. It is a new stage in the evolution of education (V.C. Kulandaiswamy, 2002).

WHAT IS DISTANCE EDUCATION?

Distance education denotes a system of education where the study is not led by teachers present in classrooms but supported by counsellors and an organisation at a distance from the learners. As opposed to face-to-face education, this system uses the postal department to send lesson units, assignment and assessment. Multimedia also uses it as a supplement. The main objective of distance education is to provide an alternative method of higher education to a larger population of people who have necessary aptitude for acquiring further knowledge and for improving their competencies.

In 1961, the Central Advisory Board of Education appointed a committee to recommend the nature, scope and mode for the organisation of correspondence courses in Indian universities. The university of Delhi is the first university in India to launch distance education in the year 1962 in the name of correspondence courses. The first state open university was set up in 1982 by the Government of Andhra Pradesh, which is now known as Dr. B. R. Ambedkar Open University. The first national open university - Indira Gandhi National Open University—was established in the year 1985 by an Act of Parliament.

At present, there are over 100 Directorates/Centres for distance education in various universities apart from 10 State Open Universities and a National Open University. The growth rate of distance education (16.2%) has been particularly higher than that of the formal system (3.9%). Open/Distance education will emerge as a viable and an effective alternative to formal education providing higher education to a larger population.

The distance learning system is a unique and challenging mode of education offered at the university level. This system provides ample opportunities for those who desire to have university education at their place of work or residence. Distance education is perhaps the only way to meet the increasing demands for higher education, especially in developing countries like India.

Need for Distance Education

In view of the limitations of the formal education system the need and demand for university education has grown over the years. Distance education provides an answer to the so-called rigid formal education, opening gates of higher education to all those who desire to pursue the course of their choice while continuing their domestic responsibilities and/or employment. Therefore, distance education has become the centre of attention for many educational organisations. Recently, many innovative, flexible educational designs using the new information and communication technologies have been developed. As a result distance education is developing fast. More and more web-based courses are being offered. However, these new forms of distance education often suffer from big problems such as student dropouts, low levels of student performance etc.

Theories of Distance Education

In looking at distance education from a broader perspective, the leading theorists in the field have developed conceptual synergies. For example, Holmberg, Charles A. Wedemeyer and Michael G. Moore put the learner and his or her interaction with others at the centre of the education process. The centrality of the learner is one of the distinguishing features of distance education, and understanding this fact is essential for discerning why it is essentially different from other forms of education.

Another example of synergy is presented by the theories and models of Desmond Keegan, Otto Peters, Randy Garrison and John Anderson, which are primarily concerned with how distance education is organised and how it functions. Although these theorists do not lose sight of the centrality of the learner, they concentrate on structural issues (e.g., industrialisation) and how such issues might affect the process of teaching and learning.

Holmberg (1995) clearly placed the learner as the corner-stone of distance education by stating, "A basic general assumption is that real learning is primarily an individual activity and is attained only through an internalising process." Unmistakably, his focus here is on the learner and the learner's responsibility for learning. Nevertheless, learner accountability is not unilateral and finds its full expression in relation to the teacher's contribution to the process of education. He termed the learner-teacher relationship as "guided didactic conversation."

Holmberg presented seven postulates to clarify this concept. In these postulates, he emphasized the importance of a "personal relation" between the learner and the teacher. This theme is often lost in the midst of the discussion of current lay views of distance education, where it is represented as a "delivery system" or a "technology" or in some other similarly misguided way. The independence of the learner is the conceptual attractor to which seminal thinkers in the field point, including Wedemeyer (1981), the premier American theorist.

Wedemeyer recognised the independence of the learner and posited that such independence would be afforded to a learner by a variety of means and strategies, including anytime and anywhere learning and learner control over the pacing of the learning process. He also acknowledged the necessity for the learner to take more responsibility for learning, freeing the instructor of the "custodial" duties of teaching. But the real impact of his contribution to the theory and practice of distance education is yet to be realised.

For Wedemeyer, distance education is a distinct "non-traditional" type of education. In his book *Learning at the Back Door,* he (1981) stated, "As Moore pointed out, learning apart (physically separated) from a teacher by means of communications through print, mechanical or electronic devices implies quite a different concept of learning from that acquired in school." Thus, he put into motion an essential concept for a revolutionary approach to learning that is just beginning to be noticed by administrators and programme planners in higher education as well as those in government, business, and industry.

Building on Wedemeyer, Moore (1983) introduced the concept of "transactional distance", which defined the relationship of instructor and learner in more precise terms. He stated, "There is now a distance between learner and teacher which is not merely geographic, but educational and psychological as well." It is a distance in the relationship of the two partners in the educational enterprise. It is a 'transactional distance'. His concept of transactional distance is important because it grounds the concept of distance in education in a social science framework and not in its usual physical science interpretation. This is a significant paradigm shift of the kind described by Kuhn (1970). Since the individual learner is significant to distance education this type of education invariably involves institutional structures as well.

Aims and Objectives of Distance Education

Distance education has been in existence for the last five decades in some form or other. The following are the aims and objectives of distance education:

a) To provide higher education to all those who could not pursue earlier through formal education
b) To strike a balance between the privileged and under privileged
c) To balance inequalities between age groups
d) To make education simple and affordable
e) To extend higher education to all
f) To benefit large groups speedily and effectively
g) To expand the capacity of education in new area
h) To offer education while continuing his/her profession and family life
i) To develop multiple competencies
j) To extend education to people living in remote corners.

Thus, the aim and objective of distance education or distance teaching is to bring more number of students to higher education to enable them to acquire higher educational qualifications without being required to join as full time students.

Development of Distance Education

Distance learning is one of the significant developments in education. It is gaining popularity all over the world as a viable alternative and for extending education to more people. The policy makers as well as educationists have started realising its potential both in the developed and developing countries.

Distance education is defined as a system of education where the learner is at a distance from the teacher for most or even all the time during the teaching-learning process. It has also been defined as a method of teaching in which the student receives instructions through printed material, radio, television and other modes such as computer aided learning and study groups.

In fact, the success of distance education depends on the use of communication media. In other words modern communication media often bridges the physical distance between the teacher and the student. However, distance education has come to stay and it has become an acceptable and viable alternative system of education. The programme of the students in this system is monitored by a team of teachers. The success of the students of distance education mainly thrives on individual motivation.

There are certain significant characteristic features of distance education, viz,

- It differs from the conventional education.
- There is distance between the teacher and the student.
- Regular participation of the student is absent in distance education.
- Students are instructed by the teacher through correspondence.
- Students extensively use electronic and mass media in this system of education.
- Large number of learners irrespective of age, formal qualification, region and nationality, join distance education.
- There exists a distance education center, which not only does the organising work but also provides the support services while enabling the student undergo the learning process.

Flexibility in Distance Education

Distance education is the only alterative to provide access to education for large number. The quality of teaching in distance education is maintained by the use of best teachers for teaching purposes. Moreover, the economies of scale apply to distance teaching. With the help of mass media, the teacher in distance education, teach large number of students at a time in different parts of the country or across the globe.

The flexibility provides immense opportunity to the students to choose the courses according to their own requirements. There is no pressure on the student to complete an undergraduate course within three years; one can study according to ones own pace and convenience. Wherever more than one system is in force, the question of parity is bound to arise.

Distance education also has to face this problem of parity in respect of value with formal education. To the conservatives and the traditionalist, distance education would seem inferior to formal education and they may treat it as second-class status. But in reality distance education learners are in no way inferior to formal education students. Degrees awarded through formal education and distance education are now treated alike, at least in principle.

NKC Views on Open/Distance Learning

The National Knowledge Commission (NKC) which was constituted on 13 June 2005 as a high level advisory body to the Prime Minister of India believes that a radical reform of the system of Open and Distance Education (ODE) is imperative to achieve the objectives of expansion, inclusion and excellence in higher education. More than one-fifth of the students enrolled in higher education are in the ODE stream. There is a clear need to improve the quality of ODE and to make it more appropriate to the needs of the society.

It is important to expand opportunities in higher education through the use of technology in ODE. It would not be possible to attain the targeted gross enrolment ratio of 15 per cent by 2015 without a massive expansion in ODE. Distance education can provide access to higher education for a large number of students, including learners with special needs. With the proliferation of media like television, radio, internet, its reach can be significantly increased.

NKC's recommendations on distance education focus on creating a national ICT infrastructure for networking ODE institutions; setting up of a national education foundation to develop web-based common open resources; establishing a credit bank to effect transition to a course credit system, establishing a national education testing service for assessing ODE students;

facilitating convergence with conventional universities; set-up research foundation to support research activity in ODE; overhauling of training programmes for educators; increasing access for learners with special needs; creating a new standing committee for the regulation of ODE and finally developing a system for quality assessment. Our success in the knowledge economy hinges to a large extent on upgrading the quality of, and enhancing the access to, education.

Global Analysis of Distance Education System

A global analysis of the distance education system is presented below under two broad heads. One, the distance education system in the first world or developed countries, and the second category pertains to distance education system prevailing in the Third World countries.

Table 1.1

Distance/Open Universities in the World

S.No.	*Name of the University*	*Country*	*Year*
1.	China TV University	China	1978
2.	India's Indira Gandhi National Open University	India	1985
3.	Open University of Hong Kong	China	1990
4.	Thailand Sukhothai Thammanthirat Open University	Thailand	1978
5.	Korea National Open University	Korea	1972
6.	Tamil Virtual University	India	1999
7.	University of the Philippines Open University	Philippines	–
8.	Chiang Mai University online Learning	Thailand	–
9.	Universidad National Abierta	Venezuela	1977
10.	University of South Africa	South Africa	1873
11.	Allama Iqbal Open University	Pakistan	1974
12.	AL-Quds Open University	Jordan	1988
13.	Anadolu University	Turkey	1985
14.	Arab Open University	Jordan	2002

(Contd...)

(Contd...)

15.	Athabasca Open University	Canada	1975
16.	Baba Saheb Ambedkar Open University, Gujarat	India	1994
17.	Bangladesh Open University	Bangladesh	1962
18.	Beijing Radio and TV University	China	1978
19.	Dr.B.R.Ambedkar Open University	India	1982
20.	Global Open University	Zambia	2002
21.	Hanoi Open University	Vietnam	1993
22.	Karnataka Open University	India	1996
23.	National Distance Learning University, Madrid	Spain	-
24.	Raja Bhoj Open University - Madhya Pradesh	India	1991
25.	Massey University	New Zealand	-
26.	Nalanda Open University	India	1987
27.	National Open University of Nigeria	Nigeria	1983
28.	National Open University, Abuya	-	-
29.	National Open University, Chinese, Taiwan	China	1987
30.	Netaji Subhas Open University	India	1997
31.	The Open Polytechnic of New Zealand	New Zealand	1946
32.	The Open University of Sri Lanka	Sri Lanka	1981
33.	U.K. Open University, Milton Keynes	UK	1969
34	Thompson Rivers University (TRU) Open Learning (TRU-OL)	Canada	—
35.	Tianjin TV University	China	—
36.	UP Rajarishi Tondon Open University	India	1998
37.	Universitad Nacinal Aberta (Open University)	Canada	1977
38.	Universities Terbuka	Indonesia	2000
39.	University of Air, Japan	Japan	1985
40.	Uttranchal Open University	India	2006
41.	Vardhman Mahaveer Open University	India	1987
42.	Wahasan Open University	Malaysia	-
43.	Yashwantra Chavan Maharashtra Open University	India	1989
44.	Yunran Radio and TV University	China	-
45.	Zambian Open University	Zambia	2002

(Contd...)

(Contd...)

46.	Zimbabwe Open University	Zimbabwe	1992
47.	Open University, Australia	Australia	-
48.	Open University of Israel	Israel	1974
49.	Open University of Sudan	Sudan	2002
50.	Open University of Tanzania	Tanzania	1992
51.	Open University, Netherlands	Netherlands	1984
52.	Open University, Tripali, Libya	Libya	1987
53.	Payame Noor University	Iran	1988
54.	Pt. Sunder Lal Sharma Open University	India	-
55.	Shanghai TV University	China	1960
56.	Sichuan Radio and TV University	China	1979
57.	Sukhothai Thammathirate Sichuan Radio and TV University	Thailand	1978
58.	Kota Open University, Rajasthan	India	1987
59.	Nalanda Open University	India	1987
60.	Tamil Nadu Open University	India	2002

Distance Education in the First World Countries

An especially distinct model of distance education known as the consultation model been developed by German Democratic Republic in 1950s. Currently, 30 of the 54 university level institutions offer education at a distance in the United Germany.

As a result of many changes, the University of South Africa (UNISA) had to seek a new role. In 1946 it began to teach by correspondence and in 1951 it was reconstituted to provide degree courses for external students, through open learning system. The university level distance education in USSR has a history of going back to 1926. It was given considerable boost following the end of the Second World War and in the light of experience gained it was regulated by Educational Act, 1958. The description pertains to the history of USSR before 1990.

The influence of the distance education system led the Whitlam Labour Government in 1973 to set up a Commission on the finding of a distance education system in Australia. Five Australian universities teach at distance. "School of Air", i.e. small units located in regional towns supplements correspondence courses for more than half of the primary students. The pre-service teacher training is afforded at a distance by a number of universities and colleges of advance education.

Accompanied by economic development in Japan, the year 1970 saw an increase in the number of people preferring distance education. The "University of Air" was established with the cooperation of many public and private institutions and the university started registration of students in April 1985.

In 1971, the United Kingdom Open University (UKOU) was established and it began to teach students within the few years of the founding. A number of other "Open or distance" universities had also been established in both developed and developing countries. The novelty of the UKOU is its success, which has triggered worldwide interest in initiating distance education system.

In the light of the changing needs of the people, the 1980 amendment to the Korean Constitution stipulates that the state promote lifelong education and that every citizen has the right to enjoy an equal opportunity for education according to his ability. To meet the growing demand the Air and correspondence education system was proposed in Korea followed by the establishment of "Air and Correspondence University and High School". Eighteen out of the 75 French universities had Centre of Tele Enlignment Universitaires [CTUS], with an enrolment of 15,000 in 1980.

The foundation of the correspondence programme at Illinois State University in 1984 can be taken as the beginning of distance education at the university level in the United States of America. The idea that university should take education to the general public particularly adults was reflected in growth of the extension movement. Canada's Distance Education at university level was initiated at Queen's University in the province of Ontario in 1989. Today, 20 Canadian Universities have correspondence courses or distance education departments.

Distance Education in the Third World Countires

Places like Nepal, a mountainous country where each one of the districts are officially declared a remote area is an obvious place for development of distance education. The College of External Studies (COES) has been providing secondary level education on a correspondence basis since 1956 in Papua New Guinea. In 1983, the college took an important step for setting up 18 provincial centres. At present the college offers courses for more than 9,000 students.

In Malaysia, distance education programmes are basically for providing education to teachers. The support system comes from the media service division (EMS) of the Ministry of Education. When it was established in 1972, the division incorporated educational radio section and an audio-visual aids section with a newly formed educational television section.

Allamma Iqbal Open University (AIOU) in Pakistan was formally established in 1974, as per the Open University Act [1972-80]. The AIOU multimedia system is designed to reduce social inequalities in education, to make education available to those who have not been able to take advantage of formal institutions and to help adults integrate their occupational and educational activities.

Sukkothai Thammathirat Open University (STOU) in Thailand, Bangkok enrolled the first batch of students in 1980. Temporarily housed in five buildings scattered around Bangkok, the university headquarters was opened in 1984. By the end of 1983 the university had admitted three batches of students – a total of around 20,000 covering every province of the country.

Distance education activities started in 1978 in Bangladesh. The Japanese government gave assistance to develop a school of broadcasting system. Now the government is considering organisation of an open university to meet the increasing demand for higher education.

In Sri Lanka's only two per cent of the students coming out of higher education can enter university. Others are seeking alternative vocational and the teachers training. It was to satisfy this need that the open university was started in 1980.

The main objective of secondary education in the Philippines is to help elementary school students who have no opportunity to enter high school, to return to the higher education. This programme is called "Distance Learning Delivery System" and was launched in 1983.

In Indonesia, as the current university system is no longer able to meet the increasing demand for higher education, an open university has been established and over 15,000 students were accommodated by this new system.

The most recent distance education programme in Afghanistan is the distance training programme for teacher educators, which provides master's level programme. Already a general system of distance education is being implemented through radio and television.

The concept of distance education is used to denote a wide range of learning strategies, referred differently in different countries such as:

1) Correspondence Education (most of the countries including India)
2) Home Study (North America and Europe)
3) Independent Study (North America)
4) External Studies
5) Open Learning
6) Open University
7) Off-Campus Studies (Australia)
8) Extra Mural Studies (New Zeeland)
9) Education at a Distance (Spanish Speaking Countries)
10) Tele Enlignment (France)
11) Fern Universitat (Germany).

The South Asian region comprises seven countries: Bangladesh, Bhutan, India, Maldives, Nepal, Pakistan and Sri Lanka. The combined population of these countries is more than one billion-approximately one-fifth of the world's population (Haub and Kent, 1988).

Spiralling population growth is placing even more pressure on governments of the region in their efforts to provide adequate resources, both human and physical, to meet the escalating demand for education and training.

To provide universal education through conventional systems (Sharma, 1989) governments have to search for cheaper, more efficient ways to provide fair and equitable access to education. It is therefore not surprising that governments in the region have been increasingly attracted to distance education.

Open universities are already well established in India, Pakistan, and Sri Lanka. The governments of Bangladesh and

Nepal are actively considering the development of open universities, while the governments of Bhutan and the Maldives have initiated plans to expand their currently limited distance education operations.

Commonwealth of Learning (COL)

An important landmark on the development of distance education in the Commonwealth countries has been the establishment of Commonwealth of Learning (COL) in 1988 at Vancouver in Canada at the instance of Commonwealth Ministers of Education and Commonwealth heads of governments. It has contributed considerably in popularising the distance education system and is also advocating the need for the improvement of the quality of course materials, staff development and training and dual mode - a part of the course to be covered by face-to-face teaching and the rest through the distance mode.

During the XV world conference of the International Council for Distance Education (ICDE) held in Bangkok in November, 1992 the presidents of ICDE and the Commonwealth of Learning signed an agreement to act jointly so as to encourage and facilitate research in distance education.

Distance Education in India

At the time of independence in 1947, there were 19 universities in India. It had increased to 186 during 1990-91. The number of affiliated colleges in India stood at 7.10 thousand during 1990-91. The enrolment in higher education during 1990-91 was 44,25,247. There are 18 central universities, 300 state universities, 16,885 colleges are giving higher education, 99.54 lakhs students are enrolled in the colleges.

Since, independence the problem of greater demand for higher education was receiving the attention of the Government of India. The population explosion further aggravated the demand for higher education. It became impossible for the formal system to meet the growing demand. Therefore, the Government of India planned to introduce the correspondence course on an experimental basis in one of the universities in India. The University of Delhi came forward to do it in 1962.

The University Grants Commission attributed the following reasons for the adoption of the system of correspondence education in India and identified the following categories of students who would benefit out of it:

1. People staying in remote area
2. People who want to continue their higher education in their own field or in new ones.
3. People who discontinued their studies for financial or other reasons.
4. People who discontinued their studies due to lack of motivation earlier but developed interest later.
5. People who for some reasons do not wish to join the regular college but wish to pursue their higher studies.

The distance education system was formally inaugurated in India by the then Union Education Minister Dr. K.L. Shrimali. On that occasion he put forth the following objectives for introducing this system:

a) Imparting efficient and less expensive higher education in the context of national development of India.
b) To provide facilities to peruse higher education to all qualified and willing persons who could not join regular university courses due to personal and economic reasons or because of their inability to get admission in a regular college; and
c) To provide opportunities of academic pursuits to educated citizen through correspondence institute without disturbing their employment.

As far as India is concerned distance education is offered through three forms viz., (a) External Registration (b) Correspondence (c) Open Universities. Of the three categories the first may be compared to private study about which the university does not hold any responsibility whereas the other two categories, the universities hold the responsibility to admit the students and award them degree or diploma.

Though, this system of education originated in India in the early 1960s, it gained momentum only in the 1970s and 1980 as number of traditional universities came forward to offer distance education courses. The University Grants Commission prescribed the guidelines to these institutions. Humanities subjects were offered through the correspondence education in the beginning and later, Social Science, Commerce, Law, Mathematics, Education and Science subjects were included. Thirty-six universities and four deemed universities offered distance education and in 1992, there were 41 conventional universities, including four deemed universities offering distance education to 4,54,000 students. There are 15 institutes in the northern region, 16 in the southern region, three in the eastern region and seven in the central and western regions.

The Central Advisory Board of Education in its 28th meeting in January 1961, noted the observation of the Planning Commission, and recommended that detailed studies for launching correspondence courses be made by a small committee before a final decision is taken. Accordingly Union Ministry of Education appointed an expert Committee under the Chairmanship of D.S. Kothari, the then Chairman of the University Grants Commission, to work out the relevant details and prepare the scheme of correspondence courses.

The population of our country increases day by day by leaps and bounds. Provision of higher education to all is not possible through formal education system. For a country like India, distance education is a necessity and its potential needs to be fully exploited. In doing this, we need to look at some of the problems still faced by distance education and chalk-out a future course of action. On the advice of the Kothari Commission, Correspondence Education was started in 1962. The Central Advisory Board of Education (CABE) had recommended that all major states should have their own open universities.

The distance education system has spread its network widely in all possible directions; several traditional universities have stepped in and started providing correspondence education. The University of Delhi was first to establish the distance education institution. Between 1970 and 1980 about 19 universities introduced this form of education which proved a major thrust to the development of distance education in the country.

It took about nine years for the system to get popularity and wide acceptance in India and therefore, in 1971 only the Punjab and Himachal Pradesh Universities started it. In the subsequent year 1972 the Sri Venkateswara University in Andhra Pradesh had instituted this non-formal education followed by the Central Institute of English and Foreign Languages (CIEFL) at Hyderabad (1973), the University of Patna (1973) Bhopal, Utkal and Bombay (1975).

The following universities viz., Maduari Kamaraj, Jammu-Kashmir and Rajasthan started correspondence education courses in 1976. Osmania and Kerala Universities (1977), the Allahabad University (1978), the Annamali and Udaipur Universities (1979), the University of Madras (1982), Bharathiyar University (1991) and Barathidasan University (1992) joined the other universities in providing distance education in India. It is to be noted here that distance education has made rapid progress in a short period in the southern region than in the northern region during 1975-76 to 1987-88.

The establishment of open universities to spread education through correspondence is a recent phenomenon in the Indian context. The United Kingdom is the pioneer in the field of open university system. It founded its open university in 1969. It received world wide attention. Walter Perry, the first Vice-Chancellor of UK Open University, took a statistical survey in 1984 and observed that there were about 756 institutions in the world offering 1969 courses to 21,00,000 students through correspondence system.

The first full-fledged and recognised open university was established in South India in Andhra Pradesh in 1982. It was established with the object of imparting education through non-formal mode without any disparity to all sections of people. Subsequently this university was renamed as "Dr.B.R. Ambedkar Open University". Following the A.P. University a number of open universities have been established in various parts of the country.

Mention has to be made about Indira Gandhi National Open University (1985) which has been very popular and recognised by all as an apex body in the open university system in India, the Kota Open University Rajasthan (1987), the Nalanda Open University, Nasik, Maharashtra (1989) and the Raja Bhoj Open University in Bhopal, Madhya Pradesh (1992). Several other states like West

Bengal, Kerala, Uttar Pradesh and Madhya Pradesh also took effective steps for establishing open universities within their jurisdiction. Thus, distance education in India which was started in 1962 saw the gradual and steady growth during the last four decades.

Indira Gandhi National Open University

The National Policy on Education (1986) of the Government of India stressed the importance of non-formal system of education to expand the educational facilities in the country. It is also proposed to strengthen distance education institutions and improve their quality. The idea of establishing an open university to offer quality education to the "much large body of population which remains outside the university system" was proposed as early as 1970 in a seminar. Co-sponsored by the Ministry of Information and Broadcasting and the UGC, following the recommendation of the seminar, the Government of India appointed an eight-member working group with G. Parthasarthy, the then Vice-Chancellor of Jawarhalal Nehru University, as Chairman.

After a decade IGNOU was established on 20 September, 1985, under an Act of Parliament. IGNOU is an apex body for open universities and distance education institutions in the country charged with the responsibilities of the promotion and coordination of the distance education system. The IGNOU Act has provide for the establishment of Distance Education Council (DEC) and Staff Training and Research Institute for Distance Education (STRIDE).

Distance Education Council

The establishment of the Indira Gandhi National Open University is a significant milestone in the development of distance education in India. The Indira Gandhi National Open University Act provided for the creation of a Distance Education Council (DEC) and the same was established in 1991 as a statutory body of the university under section 16 of the Indira Gandhi National Open University Act. The Council shall, within the framework of the policies and guidelines lay down by the Board of Management, is responsible for the open university and distance education system, and for the determination of its standards.

The Vice-Chancellor of the Indira Gandhi National Open University shall be the ex-officio Chairman; other members include representatives of the Ministry of Human Resource Development (HRD), University Grants Commission (UGC), State Open Universities, Institute of Distance/Open Education, Board of Management of Indira Gandhi National Open University, traditional formal universities and also experts from vocational (technical) education and mass media and communication.

The major functions assigned to Distance Education Council are as follows:

- Establishment of a network of open universities and distance education institutes.
- Identification of learners groups and priority areas in which distance education programme should be organised and providing necessary support for organising them.
- Training of personnel for distance education.
- Provision of financial support to open universities and distance education institutes for their development and for taking special projects.

It could be stated from the above analysis on the growth and development of distance education in the world and India that the underlying causes for introduction and development of distance education are demographic, socio-economic and individual aspirations. It has helped countries to lessen the pressure of growing demand for higher education. It has also helped to a great extent the in-service people to acquire higher education.

Thus, distance education has become a panacea for all the inadequate infrastructure problems of formal education. As far as Tamil Nadu is concerned, all major universities offer distance education, the details of which are provided in the following paragraphs.

Distance Education in Tamil Nadu

Distance education has made considerable impact on society. Even though there are certain limitations in the system, it has been accepted as a viable alternative for formal education. The population explosion in India has necessitated the states to provide education to all. Distance education has grown as a complementary to the formal education system. Further, it is considered as a boon for enhancing the standard of living of people.

Table 1.2.

Distance Teaching Institutions in Tamil Nadu

Sl.No	*Name of the Distance Teaching Institute*	*Year of Establishment*
1.	Institute of Correspondence Course and Continuing Education, Madurai Kamaraj University, Madurai	1971
2.	Directorate of Distance Education, Annamalai University, Chidambaram	1979
3.	Institute of Distance Education, University of Madras, Chennai	1981
4	Directorate of Distance Education, Alagappa University, Karaikudi	1992
5	School of Distance Education, Mother Teresa Women's University, Kodaikanal	1988
6	Centre of Distance Education of Bharathiyar University, Coimbatore	1992
7	School of Distance Education of Bharathidasan University, Coimbatore	1992
8	Directorate of Distance Education, Manonmaniam University, Tirunelveli	1994
9	Directorate of Distance Education, Periyar University, Salem	2002
10	Directorate of Distance Education, Tamil Nadu Agricultural University	2005

Socially speaking the backward class and the poorer section of the society have benefited much through this system. Under this system education is taken to the doorsteps of both rural and urban students. Since the system is simple, the students in rural areas do not find any difficulty in getting admission. Economically speaking the distance education system is cost- effective and therefore serves as a source of revenue to the universities. As far as possible, most of the directorate of distance education diverts major share of its revenue to the main university. It is an undenying fact that the conventional universities have to depend upon the income of the distance education institutes for the overall maintenance of the university.

The impact of distance education is reflected in every field. It serves the need of people irrespective of caste, creed, culture, employed, unemployed, male/female, rural/urban and tribal.

ADVANTAGES AND LIMITATIONS OF THE SYSTEM

Advantages of Distance Education

The distance education system is considered as a boon to many sections of the society since it provides an opportunity:

- To the in-service people to continue their higher education while in service for career advancement.
- To the unemployed youth to pursue higher education required for employment.
- To those already employed to study further to enhance knowledge and skills for better employment.
- To the prisoners and the handicapped people to rehabilitate and to make them live independently.
- To those dropouts from regular colleges to continue their education through the open university system as there is no age limit for pursuing distance education course.
- To the employed women and housewives to pursue their education for employment or social status.
- To the people in military service for effective utilisation of their leisure time on education and acquire additional diploma/degree.
- To the aged and retired persons to continue their interest in education in the field of their interest.

Limitations of Distance Education

Since a cross-section of people enrol in the system, it is difficult for the institution to pay personal attention to each of the student. There is no uniformity in the content and style of the study materials of different universities. Each university's lesson has its own style and standard of language. As the institutions are not quite sure of how many students would make use of the study centres they are poorly maintained without the necessary reference books, latest video equipments, etc.

CHALLENGES TO DISTANCE EDUCATION

Distance education faces numerous challenges like copyright, intellectual property rights, technology issues, digital divides, assessment, retention rates, resistance, faculty workload and compensation, legitimacy issues and dropouts. Of all the challenges, dropout in distance education tops the list requiring immediate attention of university administration. To minimise the dropout there is need for streamlining the administration process and evolving student-friendly distance education.

DROPOUT PROBLEMS IN DISTANCE EDUCATION

Dropout in distance education system means that a student who enrolled in the institute withdraws without completing the course for various reasons. Sometimes the student discontinues their studies due to the poor assistance rendered by the institutes. A study conducted into the dropout problem of distance education students in India by Khan shows that it was 29.92 per cent in 1981. As far as Tamil Nadu is concerned it was 51.2 per cent in 1982.

A higher incidence of dropout rate is observed in distance education than in conventional system (Chander, 1985). dropouts' rate in open university per course average is around 21% (Kennedy et.al. 1976). At the Fernuniversitat in Germany almost 50 per cent of their students fail to complete their first year (Millard 1982).

The dropout problem should not be looked into in isolation from the point of the students. The problem is experienced in almost all the institutions resulting in huge wastage of expenditure, time and effort on the part of the administration; also only very few realise that due to lack of quality and proper service, many of the learners drop out of the system without completing the course. For instance, in 1981, 29.92 per cent of the learners dropped out of the 11 major distance education institutes of the country. So it is high time that some introspection of the system is attempted for reducing the drop- out percentage (Khan, 1985).

According to Hathway (1978), "completion rates of those who are enrolled in open university studies are frequently low. In fact, lack of learning skills is one of the major causes for dropouts and failure in the higher education. The survival of the open university and its attainment of credibility much depend on maintaining the least dropout rate. It is needless to mention that there is no gainsaying in the fact that the prospect for the dropout is bleak (Perry 1976).

What is the type of persons dropping? Can we reduce the dropout rate? These questions figure time and again in many studies that were conducted in this area on the assumption that the number of dropouts could be reduced if we learn why learners abandoned the education system in favour of something else. Although the dropout problem for the distance education is an acknowledged fact, it can also be a very serious problem in conventional university. Studies of distance education systems have frequently been criticised on the ground that their dropout rates are unacceptable (Keegan).

The dropout problem is currently recognised as a significant educational and social problem about which practitioners, policy makers and the general public have expressed more concern. Therefore, a study on this vital issue was planned in universities in Tamil Nadu. Since, three universities only extended the cooperation for data collection a detailed study on, dropout was conducted on data obtained from these three universities.

IDE-University of Madras, Chennai

Madras, now re-named as Chennai, the capital of Tamil Nadu, had attained its glory and popularity during the regime of the British East India Company. The Woods Dispatch of 1854 lay down that the universities were to be set up in the three premier towns of Madras, Bombay and Calcutta. Accordingly, the University of Madras came into existence in 1857 with just two departments. New branches and research departments were created during the last 150 years of existence, and at present it has 70 departments of study and research.

The Institute of Distance Education (IDE), University of Madras known till 2004 as the Institute of Correspondence Education (ICE), was established in 1981. The IDE offers various need-based undergraduate and postgraduate courses. In the regular stream candidates with requisite educational qualification as adopted all over the country for higher education are admitted.

For admission into the first degree course a pass in Higher Secondary/PUC/Intermediate/Pre-Degree Examination or equivalent an examination is the prescribed minimum qualification as in the case of admission of candidates to affiliated colleges.

The open university system introduced in 1985 is intended to provide educational opportunities to those who aspire for higher education without any basic qualification, and for admission under this scheme one must have completed 18 years of age as on 1 July. The candidate is subjected to an entrance test to make sure that he/she has the required literacy level to cope with the degree course.

The number of students stood at 8,000 during the inaugural year. It is a matter of pride that today the institute of distance education has 1.5 lakh learners and 82 courses offered by the Institute of Distance Education.

DDE — Bharathidasan University, Tiruchirappalli

Bharathidasan University located in Tiruchirappalli, Tamil Nadu, India, is both a nationally and internationally well-known public higher education institution, supported by the University Grants Commission (India) and has been accredited with a five-star status of grade A, the highest rating, by the National Assessment and Accreditation Council (NAAC). The 16 schools and 47 departments and centres of the university also conduct research in addition to teaching. The university awards Bachelors, Masters and Ph.D. degrees in a wide range of study disciplines such as Engineering, Management, Sciences and Arts to qualified candidates.

The university also provides education through distance mode. The Centre for Distance Education (CDE) of Bharathidasan University (BARD) was established in the year 1992, originally intended to cater to the students of the university area, for those who could not enter the regular colleges for higher studies. The centre for distance education was extended to cover all the four southern states and union territory, viz., Tamil Nadu, Kerala,

Andhra Pradesh, Karnataka, and Pondicherry. Personal Contact Programme Centres (PCP) is located in 21 towns/cities. There are more than 14,000 students on the roll. The CDE offers as many as 66 programmes including 14 UG, 24 PG, & Diploma/PG Diploma and M.Phil. programmes.

DDE — Madurai Kamaraj University, Madurai

The Madurai Kamaraj University is a state university, established in 1966 by the Government of Tamil Nadu. It is recognised and funded by UGC and it is also a member of the Association of Indian Universities. It has been reaccredited by NAAC with grade 'A'.

The Institute of Correspondence Course and continuing Education was started in 1971. In 1996, it was renamed as the Directorate of Distance Education and has been recognised by the Distance Education Council (DEC), New Delhi. It has student strengths of about 1.20 lakhs. There are 35 spot admission centres and 80 study centres outside Tamil Nadu across the country and 12 study centres outside the country. The university was accorded the status of "Universities with Potential for Excellence", a status conferred by the University Grants Commission so far on nine such Universities in the country.

Special Features of the DDE of Madurai Kamaraj University

- Twenty-nine spot admission centres located in Tamil Nadu.
- Face-to-face teaching for 56 hours/per year/per student at 11 centres in Tamil Nadu.
- Practical training imparted at professional institutions for computer courses, M.Sc. (Phy. & Chem.) and BTHM Courses.
- Admissions made twice a year - Academic and Calendar Year streams.
- Information centres functioning at 15 places in Tamil Nadu.
- Those who have discontinued their studies under semester or non-semester in any university may continue with a year exemption.

- Those who want to study an additional degree may also do so.
- Students who are diploma (3 years) holders through polytechnics may also join in the degree courses.
- Besides printed course materials, contact classes at selected centres are arranged on Saturdays and Sundays in Tamil Nadu.
- Spot admission is available at the office of the Director and at all the 29 admission centres in Tamil Nadu.
- The Department of Adi Dravidar and Harijan Welfare, Tamil Nadu Government, offers scholarship to SC/ST students under the regular scheme.
- Tuition fee exemption for blind, deaf and dumb.

Need and Scope of the Study

This study on dropout was envisaged to understand the problems for dropout in distance education, and suggest measures to prevent or minimise the dropout rate. For wisdom lies not merely in dealing with the existing dropouts but in ensuring that dropout problem doesn't occur in future and all distance education system in India maintains maximum retention.

The magnitude of the problem of wastage due to dropout in universities varies from country to country. The emphasis of this study is on identifying the underlying causes and factors that lead to the process of dropping out the learners in distance education. What are the factors that hinder the learners to pursue their studies? How can one identify the potential dropouts that preventive measure can be taken to retain them till their successful completion of the course.

This study seeks to answer the above questions. Maybe even a partial answer will be helpful to throw light on some of the critical issues for policy makers so that recourses are conserved properly and learners entering the distance education get the expected benefit of acquiring degree/diploma required for their employment and/or career advancement. As per the review of literature, almost all the institutions face the dropout problem.

What are the factors that are responsible for the phenomenon of dropouts from distance education? If these factors are identified and remedial steps are undertaken, the number of dropouts can be reduced. The focus on dropouts in this study are based on the well known maxim "prevention is better than cure".

This study was undertaken with the following objectives:

1. To study the influence of psychological and social related factors as confronting factors for dropouts in distance education stream.
2. To analyse the educational and educational institutional related factors as a pertinent reasons for dropouts in distance education stream.
3. To analyse the employment and economic-related factors as confronting factors for dropouts in distance education stream.
4. To explore whether the family related factors and health related factors act as pertinent reasons for dropout in distance education stream.

Definition of the Terms

Distance Education (DE): The educational system that provides teaching–learning activities to a learner at a distance from teacher, educational institution is called distance education. The distance learners (DLs) and teachers are separated by physical distance. Distance education uses all possible means of communication, the postal system being only one of them. Hence, distance education includes correspondence education also.

Dropout: Distance learners abound with term such as wastage, failure, dropout and withdrawal. The term "Attrition" is used in some American and Australian writings. Rejected undergraduate students' morality and retirement are also used in the place of dropout occasionally. Since a definition helps to focus attention on an area of concern by establishing its parameters it is important that a definition of student, dropout and conceptual analysis on dropout in the area of open /distance learning system is provided here.

The dropout (Woodley et.al.1983) is used very loosely and means different things to different people. In considering the global question of student dropout (1983) have chosen to use the following measures of performance which seem most suited to the distance education.

Stagnation: Stagnation means the retention of a pupil in a given class for a period of more than one year, and is generally measured by the percentage of passes at the annual examination.

Wastage: Wastage means the premature withdrawal of children from schools and is, therefore, related to the objectives of that stage of education in connection with which the problem is being considered.

2

Studies Related to Dropouts

In the previous chapter, the role of distance education in democratising higher education along with the problems of dropouts have been presented. In the context of distance education, the dropouts occur due to various factors like personal, academic, deficiency in student support services, etc. In this chapter the related literature and relevant studies on the problems of dropouts are discussed.

Studies Conducted in India and Abroad

Educational wastage at different levels has now become an established fact. The ever-multiplying wastage rate is a dangerous to our education system in general and mankind in particular. Miller (1971) has pointed out that in some way or the other, the dropout is at a disadvantageous position compared to his peers. He may be retarded in school and below average for his grade; he may have tailed in studies; his family may live in a less favoured part of the city; his father may be employed in a status–lacking position; his parents may be lacking educational status; and so on. The dropout in this case is a marginal one.

The Mumbai Municipal Corporation conducted a study on the extent and causes of non-attendance of children in 10 different localities of Mumbai. The findings of the study revealed that (1) the incidence of non-attendance was very high in poorer areas, (2) Negligence of parents, domestic work, extreme poverty were reasons for non-attendance of children.

The investigation of Sane (1960) revealed the conditions of primary education in the educationally backward parts of the Poona Municipal Corporation. The salient findings of the study are:

1) Girls' education was neglected due to old beliefs and traditions.
2) There was ignorance about the benefits of education.
3) School courses did not attract parents.
4) Teachers failed to create an urge for education in the young minds.

Chickermane (1962) conducted a study on wastage in primary education, and stated that 40 per cent wastage is due to stagnation and failure, and only 20 per cent due to domestic circumstances and poverty.

The Maryland State Department of Education (1963) conducted a study to investigate into the causes of dropouts. The investigation revealed a high percentage of dropout (70 per cent of the mothers and 73 per cent of the fathers). The children from disturbed and poor socio-economic status suffer many psychological pressures in schools and as such this category of children is mostly the victim of premature leaving from school.

Hubba (1965) conducted a survey on dropouts and suggested measures to improve the retention rate. It was reported that the school teachers as well as the school administrators must have a sincere and genuine interest in the problem and they should help by:

1) Stressing the vocational aspects of other subjects.
2) Encouraging participation in extracurricular activities.
3) Encouraging the use of the counselling services, helping to create a strong class spirit.

The NCERT (1967) conducted a research on stagnation. The study identifies several causes for dropouts. It reveals that the rate of wastage is a more in shift system. It is less where there is a highly paid teaching staff. It is less when the pupils are trained in co-curricular activities. There is a positive correlation between the rate of dropouts and the distance of the home of the subject from the school. If the academic achievement is very high, pupils stay in and if it is very slow they drop out. Those who stay inside the school are more interested in studies than the dropouts.

Sapra C.L (1967) studied the problem of wastage and stagnation, and identified the following facts about the extent of stagnation and wastage.

a) Total instance of wastage in first eight grades was 78.35 per cent.
b) Out of the above, primary grades showed as high as 66 per cent and middle grades 26 per cent.
c) Proportion of wastage and stagnation work out to be 32.25 per cent and 46.04 per cent respectively.
d) In the post-independence period the wastage has been reduced considerably.

Mehta (1969) also conducted an experimental study entitled 'Motivating Primary Education' involving a total of 220 pupils of nine experimental schools. Pre-adolescent dependency scale and the pre-adolescent classroom trust scale were used to collect the data. The study revealed that

(1) the experiment showed a very significantly greater acquisition of the new change in their thought processes as revealed by their stories than that of controls;
(2) the experiment indicated significantly greater trust in their teachers and other classrooms situations than the controls; and
(3) the experimental schools reported some change or the other in their children than the controls.

Sharma and Sapra (1969) conducted a study on 790 dropouts and staying cases who were selected from 92 schools, selecting at least two dropouts from each grade, both in primary as well as middle schools selected for the study. For calculating the rate of dropout in 92 sampled schools, the data were gathered by the research staff of the project through different tools. The study revealed that:

1) Incidence of wastage and stagnation was more in girls than in boys.
2) More dropouts were from small size families
3) The rate of dropouts is negatively related to the qualifications and per capita income of teachers.
4) Illness, mental retardation, economic backwardness were some of the factors for dropping out from the school.

Sri Avinashilingam Home Science College, Coimbatore (1970) has conducted a study on "The problem of educating girls in the age group of 11-17 years in rural areas." The sample consisted of 500 girls from 50 villages in Coimbatore district. The primary aim was to examine the attitude and aspirations of the parents as well as girls towards education.

The major findings of the study showed that the parents of high income, small family structure with higher education and occupational levels favoured their daughters going to school. Schoolgoing girls of 11 to 17 years of age were found to have higher aspirations than those girls who dropped out of their studies midway. The socio-economic conditions were more conducive to school-going children than to the dropouts. The study pointed out that the parents of both school-going and dropout girls expressed their satisfaction towards the prevailing school conditions and facilities.

Das (1970) investigated into the causes of wastage and stagnation at the primary level education in the district of Sibsagar. His study revealed that (1) poverty and economic backwardness claimed first rank among 40 causes that were found to be responsible for wastage and stagnation at the primary stage (2) backward society and non-stimulating social environment, illiterate parents and guardians and untrained teachers claimed the 5th rank and 32nd rank respectively.

Desai (1970) also conducted a study to investigate into the causes of wastage and stagnation. The study revealed that at the elementary stage, dropsout is due to economic causes, parental indifference, repeated failure in the examinations, social habits and early marriage. To minimise the dropout rate certain measures have been put forth, such as proper guidance of parents and pupils, counselling programmes for parents, remedial reading for slow learners and under-achievers.

The Kothari Commission (1970) in their monumental work on education reported large dropout and stagnation rates during the early years of schooling. The dropout rate was the highest in the first standard.

The various causes cited by the Commission include the heterogeneity of age composition of pupils and the prevailing practice of allowing the admissions throughout the year instead of only during the beginning of the academic year. The other causes as pointed out by the Commission are the irregularity of attendance, lack of educational equipment in the school as well as with the children, overcrowded classes, unsuitable curricula and a rigid system of examination. The Commission pointed out that the teachers who used "play ways" techniques to assist in initiating children smoothly to school life helped to prevent dropouts.

William G. Spady's (1970) study on "Dropouts from higher education, an interdisciplinary review and synthesis dropout process from higher education" is examined from a variety of operation definitions and intellectual perspective. A methodological analysis, critique and synthesis of the empirical literature suggest that a more rigorous interdisciplinary approach must be attempted.

A model based on Durkheim's theory of suicide provides a fruitful vehicle for summarising a large proposition of current research and focusing future attention on the interaction between student attributes (i.e., dispositions, interests, attitudes and skills), and the influences, expectations and demands composed by various sources in the university environment. Both the academic and social systems of the university are regarded as important frameworks from which the dropout process.

Masavi (1971) carried a study on wastage and stagnation in primary education amongst the tribal of Gujarat. The sample consisted of 104 schools and 14 Ashram schools belonging to the 15 tribal development blocks in the eight tribal districts of Gujarat. The techniques used for data collection included individual and group interviews of local leaders, parents, and teachers education inspectors. The main findings of the study were:

1) The rate of wastage in the two selected base years was 39 per cent and 24 per cent respectively
2) The first grade was found to be stumbling block in the sphere of primary education
3) Ashram schools showed lower rate of wastage than panchayat schools
4) Economic backwardness was found to be the primary causes for wastage and stagnation
5) Illiterate parents, unsuitable curriculum and non-stimulating school environment were other factors.

Malcom S. Adiseshaiah (1974) pointed out in the *Indian Express Newsline* that; the curriculum was outdated and irrelevant. He described the present examination system as the Chola's era of the education system. He gives a statistical explanation about the dropouts in primary schools in Tamil Nadu, that out of the 95 per cent of children enrolled in the first standard 52 per cent dropped out before they reached the fourth standard, and about 80 per cent dropped out in the XI standard, and finally only 4 per cent stepped into college.

Khandekar (1974) carried out a study on dropouts on the socio-economic and environmental characteristics of school dropouts. The sample consisted of youth in the age group of 14-21 years, those who had been to school for some time but could not complete the secondary stage of education. The subjects were living in 10 slum areas of Bombay. The interview method was used for data collection. The study revealed that:

1) parents of the dropouts were illiterate
2) poor families
3) low girls ratio
4) poverty
5) as many as 69 per cent of dropout stopped on their own while 31 per cent on the suggestions of their parents and
6) as many as 53 per cent of dropout expressed a desire to start again.

The study of Kennedy, et.al. (1976) indicates that both within and outside the open university for the most part, presented a very general statistical description and analysis, for example, a profile of students who are most likely to drop out, and courses that have high dropout rates than other, are much debated (e.g. their motivation, age and their circumstances and financial situation).

Triwari (1979) conducted a study on 200 families in two equal sets of primary school children of Agra town. The school lists of the dropout and non-dropout were drawn randomly. The study revealed that:

1) average and large size family favour dropout
2) The least of education is available with the dropout mothers

3) the parents of dropout are significantly less educated; and
4) the dropout parents more significantly suffer from frustration.

Venkatasubramanian (1980) has extensively dealt with this problem of dropouts in his book *On education and economic development in India*. This study was carried out with a view to analyse the economic aspects of the growth of primary education in Tamil Nadu and to ascertain the private expenditure in education which helps to determine the total costs factor. It attempted to prove that education especially first level education has salient features.

The important findings of the study were that the percentage of girls enrolled in upper primary level during 1956-57 was 23.31 per cent and it increased to 35.37 per cent during 1974-75. The dropout of girls was higher than boys in all the districts. Dharmapuri district had the highest dropout rate for both boys and girls while Kanyakumari district had the lowest dropout rate.

Carr and Ledwith (1980) sought to determine the factors related to success of disadvantaged adults beginning their studies with the British Open University. They obtained questionnaires from 332 disadvantaged students, who had dropped out or failed, and a random sample of 100 who had completed their course work, and a random sample of students who were interviewed by telephone. They discovered that while only one-fourth of the disadvantageous group had received academic counselling, two-thirds of those who had dropped out expressed their desire for more academic assistance. Those who were enrolled in the arts and social sciences were more likely to cite personal or domestic problems. Those who were in mathematics, science, and technology courses cited more job-oriented reasons with employment a major difficulty.

Rekkedal's (1983) study reveals that the reasons students give to explain why they withdraw may reflect the depth of questions they were asked. When more probing questions were asked of individuals who had dropped out from the Norwegian NKI School, additional study-related reasons were revealed: "problems concerning the teaching/learning method itself, the subject matter of planning/organising of studies, dissatisfaction with the study material, the tutors' work, and turn-around time of assignments."

Medill Natriello and Pallas (1985) conducted a study on raising the standards and retaining students. They examined the potential influence of school reform, policies on the high dropout incidence, and revealed that increasing academic standards in school as a means of improving secondary school performance may encourage greater student effort and time on school work, and thus lead to a high level of achievement.

Naqash (1988) conducted a study on potential dropouts in Kashmir. The main objectives of the study were to find out the predictors of dropout. Being an experimental study it revealed that different components of treatment combined together yielded an improvement of 78.22 per cent in the gain scores of potential dropouts. Further, it has identified four main predictors of dropout incidence. The Municipal Corporation (1956) had studied the incidence of dropouts in primary school setting 7,800 children from 16 schools.

Singh (1988) investigated the extent and causes of dropout among girls in the rural schools of Chandigarh. The study found that the dropout rate of rural girl was higher at class 1 level in the primary stage compared to other classes, with this rate going down in the higher grades. The girls were generally weak in English, Mathematics and Science. Parents were unwilling to send their daughters because of domestic reasons. Muslims married off their daughters at an early age and the families were generally poor and sometime forced their daughters to support and supplement the family income by cleaning utensils. Further, lack of interest, illness and weakness in studies, stepmother, large family, parental illiteracy, parental illness and the social factors of early marriage and orthodox thinking were other causes for large dropout.

The study of G.S. Rawat (1987) for UP shows that the dropout rate for children coming from the higher socio-economic status is relatively higher than for children coming from lower economic status; this indicates the negative effect of better economic conditions on the attendance of the children.

R.V. Pandit (1989) and Ray Jognte (1989) found that unsafe conditions deterred parents from sending mature girls to co-educational schools. The dropout rate was higher among illiterate families. Unemployment created a negative attitude amongst patents. Young male teachers were a substantive cause of withdrawal of girls. Other major factors were inconvenient school timings, long distance from house, lack of proper coaching for difficult subjects and heavy curriculum at secondary level.

The cause of dropout listed in the study of Rajasthan were as follows: personal causes, poor financial conditions of the family circumstances, parental unwillingness, illiteracy of parents, illness or weakness in studies, inferiority complex, handicapped overage dropout of friend /sibling and difficulty in finding a bridegroom for a literate girl. School-related causes include non-availability of lady teachers, co-educational system and lack of interest of the teachers.

D.W. Hood (1992) investigated into the academic and non-cognitive factors affecting the retention of black men at predominantly White University. The study reveals:

(i) Eight non-cognitive factors were found to be related to the academic success of minority students.

(ii) Black minority students were less inclined to leave college contrarily but rather as a result of academic dismissal.

(iii) They attribute the high dismissal rate for Black minority students to allowing situations to get to them, not taking college seriously until late and not getting help when needed.

Edward McCaul, et al. (1992) studied the consequences of dropping out of school, high school and beyond. The purpose of this study was to examine the personal, social and economic consequences of dropping out of school. Dropout differed from graduates with no post-secondary education on many personal and social adjustment measures. Results indicate that male and female dropouts have different personal, social and economic experiences.

Josefina McDonough (1993) carried out a study of dropping out and delinquency rates. Using 69 Zip code areas in Maricopa Country, Ariz on a, drawn from the 1980 census survey tape, an attempt was made to characterise communities along dimensions that contribute to the concentration of youth and to compare rates of delinquency across communities with distinctive profiles.

Community economic variables turn out to be stronger predicators of dropout and delinquency rates than family variables.

Nayat, et al. (1992) have done major national study on a sample of 3,000 households located in the urban slums and rural areas of Delhi, Mumbai Orissa and Rajasthan. The study made a methodological contribution by

(a) having the house hold as an entry point, and

b) studying the phenomenon of non-enrolment and dropout separately.

Gender discrimination was evident in intra-household distribution of food, health care, education, play and recreation. Parents have substantially lower academic and occupational aspirations for girls and are unwilling to spend money on non-tuition costs for items such as books, uniforms, stationary, shoes, etc., because they consider girls as temporary members of the household and poor investment.

Scott Davies (1994) and Hosaka Toru (1996) conducted a follow-up survey of long absence and persistent non-attendance. In this survey, all children in elementary and junior high schools who were absent from school for more than 30 days in one school year from 1989 to 1991 in a certain city were investigated. In elementary schools, one-third of the students were absent from the school for more than 30 days even the following year, and half of them were school non-attendants. In junior high schools, half of the students who were absent from school for more than 30 days in one school year in 1989 and 1990 were also absent for more than 30 days even in the following years. And 80 per cent of them were school non-attendants. Twenty per cent of the students were also absent from school for more than 30 days in one year.

Keith Tyler-Smith (1994) studied the problem of dropout rates in e-learning programme and argued at length factors that contribute to learner dropping out, withdrawing or not completing e-learning courses. The complexity and quantum of variables identified as to the potential or actual causes of dropout rates and attrition in e-learning allow for few practical or readily applied situations. The one area where something may be done to reduce attrition is in the early stages of online courses. Cognitive overload is a likely contributor to high dropout rates.

Joy D.Teachman, Paasch and Karen Carver (1996) conducted the study of social capital and dropping out of school. A large sample of data was taken from the national educational longitudinal survey to examine the effects of various measures of social capital on the likelihood of dropping out of school early, before the 10th grade controlling for indicators of financial and human capitals of parents. Results indicate that more specific indicators of social capital (patterns of parental interaction, number of times the child changed school) could account for all of the effect of attending a catholic school, but only a fraction of the effect of family structure on leaving school early.

Moore and Kearsley (1996) have identified 12 key general design principles for successful distance education programmes. Four of them, especially related to the results of this study, are good structure, clear objectives, feedback and planned participation to increase types of interaction. Furthermore, even though participants thought they were satisfied with instructors' efforts and desires in the programme, it is not enough for them because participants stated that they could not get enough satisfactory support and feedback, especially individual feedback. Likewise, Garland (1993) studied distance education student perceptions of barriers to retention of the study. Barriers found in his study included poor learning environment, problems with institutional procedures, problems with course scheduling, problems concerning tutorial assistance, lack of clear goals, and lack of support. These problems are also mentioned by some research in the literature (Morgan & Tam, 1999; Frankola, 2001, Saba 2002; Rossett & Schafer, 2003).

Bhat (1997) in his study on the incidence of dropout among students in relation to their personal and social adjustment conducted in Kashmir has revealed that :

1) the total dropout incidence rate was found 39.64 per cent in both rural and urban habitats;
2) the high dropout incidence was found among girls students
3) dropouts and adjustment (personal, social and total) were found positively and significantly related to each other, and
4) potential dropouts and stains differ significantly in their personal, social and total adjustment.

Gomathi Mani (1998) states in her study that on female dropouts from distance education, the majority of the dropouts said they reason dropedout from the distance education stream due to lack of proper guidance from the family, lack of library facilities, lack of verity in teaching methods and academic help. Some left the course because they were transferred. She emphasized that continues research must be done on students' life situation. It will prevent the students' dropout.

Jenny Wang's (2000) study "Strategies for reducing dropout from distance education courses" aims to identify the significant characteristics of distance education students who have dropped out from the distance education programme in Taiwan. The major focus was based on the factors which might relate to the students' decisions for dropping out or staying in the distance education programmer to establish a set of strategies to reduce dropout from distance education courses. The participants in the study were undergraduate students who originally enrolled in distance education undergraduate programmer at the National Open University of Taiwan. The instrument used in this research was a questionnaire for investigating the factors of dropout or retention for distance education students, demographic variables, goal commitment, social integration and academic integration.

The recommendations as were

1. The institution should offer flexibility within units and a wide choice of units to form a course in order to maximise intrinsic motivation students.
2. Every distance learning centre should have enough staff to assist the student.

Taj Haseen's (2002) study on causes of dropouts at primary school level reveals that the rate of enrolment should be increased and dropouts should be decreased. This will not be possible unless our schools become places of attraction for joyful learning with the necessary infrastructures and dedicated teachers. Primary education has become a dream due to higher rate of dropouts. The dream of 100 per cent primary education is very hard to attain if not impossible.

Vergidis and Panagiotakopoulos (2002) conducted a study to examine the root causes of student dropouts in Hellenic Open University's postgraduate programme in Greece (neighbour country). They found that working adults' obligations are the main cause of dropping out. These obligations are especially related to workload, work commitments and family obligations. Furthermore, Tresman (2002) provided data from the 1998–2000 survey in the open university, UK.

In her study she stated that the most significant factor influencing students' decision to withdraw from online courses was lack of time. Balancing work and family obligations were other factors which also ranked high in the survey. Illness, death, divorce, house removal and job loss were also cited as reasons for dropout.

According to Linda Reneland's (2003) study most of the factors are covered by the responsibilities of course management. On second place, after private conditions, come opportunities for exchanging views. This as well as progression in course content and interaction with course management should be regarded as important when planning for and designing distance education courses. Students have expectations of not having to travel and possibilities to focus on studies in certain periods where the work situation is slow, for instance. Clear information about what is being offered is a key question in getting the right target group and avoid "drop-ins" for distance education course.

Christos Pierrakees's (2004) study shows results of a survey designed to investigate the relationship between dropout with intrinsic (student-related) factors such as sickness, work/school conflict, etc., and extrinsic (institutional-related) factors such as study methods and materials, educational approach and tutor influence. The most significant reasons they cited for dropping out were their underestimation of the actual time they had at their disposal for studying versus their other obligations, and / or unforeseen changes in their daily work environment (e.g. promotions, transfer, pregnancy, death) that affected their ability to continue with their studies. At the postgraduate level dropout the rates were significantly lower than those at the undergraduate programme.

Quinn Jocey's (2004) article "Understanding working-class a dropouts from higher education through a socio-cultural lens: cultural narratives and local contexts" focused on "dropouts" of working class students from universities. This has been identified as one of the most pressing issues for the higher education sector in UK. Findings of a major research project explore the meanings and implications of such withdrawal from higher education amongst young working class people. The dropout should be seen not just as an educational problem, but also as a manifestation of socio-cultural change. To understand dropout we need to look beyond students needs or institutional barriers to cultural narratives and local contexts. This enables us to use a sociological frame to understand the educational questions and employ the educational data to contribute to sociological debates on class. An analysis of a dropout as a self-fulfilling cultural narrative is increasingly computed as a working class as well as being a consequence of the material exigencies of working class circumstances.

Lawrence Gladieux (2005) utilised the most recent and comprehensive data available from the US department of education on students who first enrolled in post-secondary education in 1995-96, with a snapshot of the same students in 2001. The findings are revealing, if not disturbing. Among half of the students who enrolled in post-secondary education in 1995-96, more than 20 per cent of those students dropped out of their educational programmes. There are, of course many legitimate points of view about how to best support students financially. However, requiring students to assume significant financial risks so early in their educational careers poses a barrier to educational opportunity for many low-income and first-generation students.

Erman Yukselturk et al. (2006) in their study analysed the factors that affect the dropout rates in online certificate programme. Participants of the programme represented different educational background, employment, financial status, marital and family status. Some of the participants were students at different departments in universities or some of them had jobs or other responsibilities. The results of this study was limited because the focus of this study was on a certificate programme with a small number of dropout students.

The factor affecting student retention in this online certificate programme was combined into two main reasons: the learner side and the problems of the programme itself. Research states that online learners had different responsibilities and properties compared to traditional instruction. For example, learners could assume control of their learning. Increased responsibility and accountability for learning were required of online learners (McGrath, 1998). Furthermore, the findings showed that participants had many problems in finding time for the programme and some had personal problems related to their job, family or finances. Also, some participants had adaptation problems to distance education resulting in decreasing motivation gradually. The dropout reasons in the literature are online with these findings (Parker, 1995; Vergidis & Panagiotakopoulos, 2002; Arsham, 2002; Xenos & Pierrakeas & Pintelas, 2002; Saba, 2002).

Gerard Lassibille and Lucia Navarvo (2007) ask in their paper, Why do higher education students drop out? The statistical analysis was carried out in a competing risks framework. Academic preparedness was one of the major influences on student completion. Older students, who delayed entry into higher education, were more likely to drop out before graduating. An analysis provided guidance about the role that financial support played in reducing dropout rates; family characteristics were significant factors in explaining student drop-out in long programmes.

Jane Marshall (2009) in his article "Why dropouts" states why one in five students who enrol in French higher education quit without qualifying. The organisation said these thousands of young people without a university diploma or degree dropped out. Latest findings of the centre for studies and research on qualifications show that 20 per cent of students who enrolled in higher education, dropped out from their studies.

The report identified several factors:

1. Students failed to adapt to new methods of working, methods that succeeded at school did not suit university studies, with less rigorous timetable, less supervision and need for more self-discipline.
2. All the young people questioned had other interests, such as sport, culture and paid employment which had greatly increased during the past 30 years, often because it gave them a sense of independence and when the exam failure loomed, an opportunity came to drop out.

Kamla Raj's (2007) study was aimed at finding out the extent of school dropouts among girls and to know the factors responsible for low enrolment and dropout of girls in schools. A sample of 150 respondents was selected from the local Government Senior Secondary Schools of Bhawarna Block of Himachal Pradesh. The major findings revealed a significant association between family type, income and education of mothers with an incidence of dropouts. Classwise and yearwise analysis showed a decreasing trend of dropping out in the past two years. In parents' opinion, the behaviour of teachers, inappropriate teaching methods, an unsuitable curriculum, lack of child's interest in studies, low grades in class, financial strain and a girl's requirement in household work and care of siblings were important factors for low enrolment and dropout of girls in schools.

3

Research Methodology

The formulation of objectives, hypotheses, design and procedure of investigation are dealt with in this chapter. The elusive phenomenon of dropouts is persisting at all distance education institutions in the world. The review of related literature, personal inquiries and discussions with dropouts in open learning/distance education system have led to the next step of formulation of objectives and hypotheses, which is considered as a central step in any research work.

Goode and Hatt (1952) consider formulation of hypothesis as a crucial step in scientific research. According to them questions are put to the entire world in such a form that an answer can be obtained objectively. The hypotheses formed, should have conceptual reference, clear and precise, containing specific relationship between phenomena, so that it can be tested and demonstrated as either probable or not probable.

Davis (1981) states that hypotheses should serve as a guide to tactic and interpretative understanding of issues. The specific intentions of the study should be formulated as hypotheses to be subjected to statistical tests even before the formulation of objectives. It is necessary to arrive at certain objectives, personal attributes and clusters of factors, which have influenced the learners to drop out of distance education system.

Identification of Attributes

Based on the initial interaction with dropouts have been identified the following attributes for investigation. Personal Attribute that are associated with the dropouts are:

1. Age
2. Sex
3. Marital status
4. Type of family
5. Religion
6. Community
7. Place of birth
8. Educational qualification
9. University studied
10. Employment status
11. Family's annual income

Dropout Causes in Distance Education

Two major factors that are responsible for dropping out are individual factors and institutional factors.

Individual Factors

1. Psychological factors
2. Family-related factors
3. Social-related factors
4. Health-related factors
5. Educational factors
6. Employment-related factors
7. Economic-related factors

Psychological factors

1. No intention for further study
2. Less retention/memory power
3. Fear of failure

4. Inferiority complex
5. Teasing by others

Family-related factors

1. More time spent on children's care
2. Heavy domestic work
3. More family expenditure
4. Lack of motivation from family members
5. Limited income

Social-related factors

1. Too much family restrictions
2. Marriage
3. Religious restriction
4. Unwillingness of spouse to continue study

Health factors

1. Physical disability
2. Chronic illness
3. Children's ill health
4. Elders' or family member(s), ill health

Educational factors

1. High standard syllabus
2. No library facility
3. Lack of job opportunity
4. Difficulties in comprehension of the subjects
5. Absence of peer group for discussion/clarification
6. Examination syllabus is very high

Employment-related factors

1. Heavy workload in the office
2. Promotion and consequent pressure of work
3. Transfer within the existing organisation
4. Transfer to another place
5. New additional responsibility in the office

Economic-related factors

1. High tuition fees is high
2. Inability to continue due to economic conditions of family
3. Examination fees failure to pay
4. Unavailability of scholarship

Institutional Factors

1. Delay in receipt of study materials
2. High tuition fees
3. No proper response to communication
4. Not providing study materials on time
5. Non-receipt of study materials during the course period
6. Inadequate library facilities and student support services

Operational Definition of Dropout

The term 'dropout' for the purpose of the present study is identified as those who:

- Enrolled for their course during the academic year 2000-2001.
- Did not pay the tuition fees after the first term or year.
- Did not pay the examination fees.
- Paid the examination fees but did not attend the examinations.
- University served a discontinuation order.

Objectives of the Study

This study has been planned on the following objectives:

1. To study the influence of psychological and social-related factors as a confronting factor for dropouts in distance education.
2. To analyse the educational and institutional-related factors as pertinent reasons for dropouts in distance education.
3. To analyse the employment and economic-related factors as confronting factors for dropouts in distance education.
4. To explore the role of family-related factors and health-related factors as a pertinent reason for dropouts in distance education.

Hypotheses

Null hypotheses are postulated since there are no comparable studies reported in this country and elsewhere.

1. There will be no significant association between psychological factors and the following personal attributions such as Age, Sex, Employment, Marital status, Type of family, Religion, Community, Educational qualification, Place of Birth, Annual Income and University studied.
2. There will be no significant association between family-related factors and personal attributions.
3. There will be no significant association between social-related factors and personal attributions.
4. There will be no significant association between health-related factors and personal attributions.
5. There will be no significant association between educational-related factors and personal attributions.
6. There will be no significant association between employment-related factors and personal attributions.

7. There will be no significant association between economic-related factors and personal attributions.
8. There will be no significant association between institutional-related factors and the personal attributions.

Research Design

Descriptive survey studies are concerned with describing the characteristics of a particular individual or of a group (Kothari,1990). Considering the objectives, hypotheses and type of sample and the very nature of the problem, a descriptive survey design was chosen. Furthermore, this study focuses on the description of various causes and the consequences of the learners who had dropped out from the distance education stream of three universities, and therefore, a descriptive survey design was preferred to other research designs.

Distribution of Samples

For this study, learners who dropped out in the distance education system were from select three universities were they were admitted during the academic year 2000–2001. The dropouts were decided on the following criteria:

- Those who did not pay the tuition fees after the first term or first year.
- Those who did not pay the examination fees.
- Those who the fees but did not attend the examinations.
- Those who were served a discontinuation order by the university.

On the basis of the above four conditions, all those who had dropped out during the academic year (2000-2001) were considered as sample for the study. For the study, the Directorate of Distance Education attached to Annamalai University, Chidambaram, University of Madras, Chennai, Madurai Kamaraj University, Madurai and Bharathiyar University, Coimbatore in Tamil Nadu were selected. But Annamalai University and Bharathiyar University did not extend cooperation to give the list of dropouts and other data. So, two other universities (Bharathidasan University and Alagappa University) were chosen for data collection. But finally, only three universities (University of Madras, Madurai Kamaraj University and Bharathidasan University) cooperated and provided data related to this study.

The universe for this study represents the distance learners (UG and PG) enrolled in the three universities during the year 2000-01. From the total population of the dropouts in these three universities, it was estimated to collect at least 300 samples from each university by stratified random sampling method, so as to have a total of 900 samples. The required data for the study were collected through mailing (postal) questionnaires. Three hundred questionnaires were sent to the respondents in each university. But only 316 filled-in the questionnaires from all the three universities were received and these 316 questionnaires were analysed for this study.

The tools required for the investigation were constructed at different stages. At the first stage, was reviewed the literature available in the libraries and website, which has helped in identifying the relevant variables concerned with the study. A workshop earlier on "Reasons for dropouts from the distance education" was conducted by the author among the distance educators/educationists. Based on the input received from the workshop, tools for the study were prepared. Valuable suggestions given by the faculties were streamlined and organised as a systematic questionnaire.

The prepared questionnaire was initially given to five field expert professors who are associated with educational research and development with a request to scrutinise the questionnaire for its validity. The professors, after reviewing the complete questionnaire, gave some suggestions and then the questionnaire was modified with addition/deletion of few items. Thus the content validity of the questionnaire was ensured.

Analysis of Data

After collection of the data, the data was analysed by descriptive analysis to find out the reasons for dropouts with regard to their socio-economic background of the learners. Chi-square techniques were made use of to verify the hypotheses and derive the most pertinent reasons for dropouts. The above-said analyses were applied with regard to the learners who dropped out from the distance education stream.

4

Analysis and Interpretation of Data

In the present study, the data collected in relation to dropouts in distance education programme were analysed based on the objectives and hypotheses of the study. The data has been subjected to the following approach, namely, inferential and descriptive analysis. Inferential statistical technique was applied to derive the pertinent reasons for dropouts.

The descriptive analysis was applied to find out the reasons for dropouts with regard to their socio-economic background of the learners. Inferential statistical technique was applied to derive the pertinent reasons for dropouts.

Inferential Analyses on Sample

Hypothesis 1

There will be no association between psychological factors and personal attributes, like age, sex, marital status, type of family, religion, community, place of birth, educational qualification, university studied, employment status and family's annual income.

Sub-hypothesis 1.1

There is no association between students' age and psychological factors as a reason for the dropouts.

As per Table 4.1, the P-value is significant at 0.05 per cent level between the student's age and the psychological factors as a reason for the dropouts from the distance education institution. Therefore, the null hypothesis is rejected.

Table 4.1
Chi-square Test for Association between Age and Psychological Factors

Psychological factors	*Age Group*					
	18 - 22	*23 - 27*	*Above 27*	*Total*	*Chi Square Value*	*P-Value*
Lack of Interest	11 (11.7)	49 (52.1)	34 (36.2)	94		
Lack of Memory	8 (9.0)	47 (52.8)	34 (38.2)	89		
Fear of Failure	17 (34.0)	22 (44.0)	11 (22.0)	50	18.997	0.014*
Inferiority Complex	10 (20.4)	21 (42.9)	18 (36.7)	49		
Others	5 (15.2)	14 (42.4)	14 (42.4)	33		
Total	51	153	111	315		

* Significant at 0.05 per cent level

It has come to be known that the students in the age group 18-22, 23-27 and above 27 were having different reasons as a psychological factor for the dropouts. The table reveals that the age group 23-27 is more influenced by the psychological factors as a reason for the dropouts than the age group above 27.

***Sub-hypothesis* 1.2**

There is no association between students gender and psychological factors as a reason for the dropouts.

As per Table 4.2, the P-value is greater than 0.05 levels; there is no association between the students' gender and the psychological factors as a reason for the dropouts from the distance education institution. Therefore, the null hypothesis is accepted.

It has come to be known that males and females have a similar kind of psychological factors as a reason for the dropout.

Table 4.2

Chi-square Test for Association between Sex and Psychological Factors

Psychological factors	*Sex*				
	Male	*Female*	*Total*	*Chi Square Value*	*P-Value*
Lack of Interest	59 (62.8)	35 (29.2)	94		
Lack of Memory	63 (70.8)	26 (29.2)	89		
Fear of Failure	29 (58.0)	21 (42.0)	50	3.225	0.520@
Inferiority Complex	29 (59.2)	20 (40.8)	49		
Others	20 (60.6)	13 (39.4)	33		
Total	200	115	315		

@ Denotes not significant

Table 4.3

Chi-square Test for Association between Marital Status and Psychological Factors

Psychological factors	*Marital status*				
	Married	*Unmarried*	*Total*	*Chi Square Value*	*P-Value*
Lack of Interest	45 (47.9)	49 (52.1)	94		
Lack of Memory	38 (42.7)	51 (57.3)	89		
Fear of Failure	21 (42.0)	29 (58.0)	50	7.967	0.092@
Inferiority Complex	24 (49.0)	25 (51.0)	49		
Others	23 (69.7)	10 (30.3)	33		
Total	151	164	315		

@ Denotes not significant

Sub-hypothesis 1.3

There is no association between marital status of the dropouts and psychological factors as a reason for the dropouts.

As per Table 4.3, the P-value is greater than 0.05 levels; there is no association between the marital status of the dropout and the psychological factors as a reason for the dropouts from the distance education institution. Therefore, the null hypothesis is accepted.

Psychological factors do not figure between the married and unmarried as a reason for the dropouts.

Sub-hypothesis 1.4

There is no association between the family type of the dropout and the psychological factors as a reason for dropout.

Table 4.4: Chi-square Test for Association between Type of Family and Psychological Factors

Psychological Factors	*Type of family*				
	Nuclear	*Joint*	*Total*	*Chi Square Value*	*P-Value*
Lack of Interest	28 (29.8)	66 (70.2)	94		
Lack of Memory	26 (29.2)	63 (70.8)	89		
Fear of Failure	15 (30.0)	35 (70.0)	50	3.909	0.418@
Inferiority complex	13 (26.5)	36 (73.5)	49		
Others	15 (45.5)	18 (54.5)	33		
Total	97	218	315		

@ Denotes not significant

As per Table 4.4, the P-value is greater than 0.05 levels; there is no association between the type of family of the dropout and the psychological factors as a reason for the dropouts from the distance education institution. Therefore, the null hypothesis is accepted.

It is observed that the type of family does not play a major role as a reason for the dropouts.

Sub-hypothesis 1.5

There is no association between the religion of students and the psychological factors as a reason for the dropouts.

Table 4.5: Chi-square Test for Association between Religion & Psychological Factors

Psychological factors	*Religion*					
	Hindu	*Muslim*	*Christian*	*Total*	*Chi Square Value*	*P-Value*
Lack of Interest	60 (63.8)	17 (18.1)	17 (18.1)	94		
Lack of Memory	52 (58.4)	23 (25.8)	14 (15.7)	89		
Fear of Failure	28 (56.0)	16 (32.0)	6 (12.0)	50	6.530	0.588@
Inferiority complex	30 (61.2)	10 (20.4)	9 (18.4)	49		
Others	24 (72.7)	5 (15.2)	4 (12.1)	33		
Total	194	71	50	315		

@ Denotes not significant

As per Table 4.5, the P-value is greater than 0.05 levels; there is no association between the religion of students and the psychological factors as a reason for the dropouts from the distance education institution. Therefore, the null hypothesis accepted.

It is observed that the student's religion does not play a vital role as a reason for the dropouts.

Sub-hypothesis 1.6

There is no association between the community of students and the psychological factors as a reason for the dropouts.

Table 4.6

Chi-square Test for Association between Community and Psychological Tactors

Psychological factors	*Community*						
	B.C	*M.B.C*	*SC/ST*	*OC*	*Total*	*Chi Square Value*	*P - Value*
Lack of Interest	39 (41.5)	30 (31.9)	18 (19.1)	7 (7.4)	94		
Lack of Memory	46 (51.7)	22 (24.7)	14 (15.7)	7 (7.9)	89		
Fear of Failure	24 (48.0)	10 (20.0)	11 (22.0)	5 (10.0)	50	10.808	0.545 @
Inferiority complex	20 (40.8)	11 (22.4)	10 (20.4)	8 (16.3)	49		
Others	18 (54.5)	6 (18.2)	8 (24.2)	1 (3.0)	33		
Total	147	79	61	28	315		

@ Denotes not significant

As per Table 4.6, the P-value is greater than 0.05 levels; there is no association between the student's community and the psychological factors as a reason for the dropouts from the distance education institution. Therefore, the null hypothesis is accepted.

It is observed that the student's community, namely, Backward, Most Backward, Scheduled/Scheduled tribes or other communities does not play a major role as a reason for the dropouts in the distance education stream.

Sub-hypothesis 1.7

There is no association between the place of birth of the dropouts and the psychological factors as a reason for the dropouts.

Table 4.7

Chi-square Test for Association between Place of Birth and Psychological Factors

Psychological factors	*Place of Birth*				
	Urban	*Rural*	*Total*	*Chi Square Value*	*P-Value*
Lack of Interest	50	44	94		
	(53.2)	(46.8)			
Lack of Memory	49	40	89		
	(55.1)	(44.9)			
Fear of Failure	26	24			
	(52.0)	(48.0)	50	1.628	0.803@
Inferiority complex	29	20			
	(59.2)	(40.8)	49		
Others	15	18			
	(45.5)	(54.5)	33		
Total	169	146	315		

@ Denotes not significant

As per Table 4.7, the P-value is greater than 0.05 levels; there is no association between the place of birth of the dropouts and the psychological factors as a reason for the dropouts from the distance education institution. Therefore, the null hypothesis is accepted.

Psychological factors do not figure in the place of birth of the dropout, whether urban or rural, as a reason for dropouts.

Sub-hypothesis 1.8

There is no association between the student's educational qualification and their psychological factors as a reason for the dropouts.

As per Table 4.8, the P-value is greater than 0.05 levels; there is no association between the student's educational qualification and the psychological factors as a reason for the dropouts from the distance education institution. Therefore, the null hypothesis is accepted.

Table 4.8

Chi-square Test for Association between Educational Qualifications and Psychological Factors

Psychological factors	*Educational qualifications*				
	U.G	*P.G*	*Total*	*Chi Square Value*	*P-Value*
Lack of Interest	57 (60.6)	37 (39.4)	94		
Lack of Memory	53 (59.6)	36 (40.4)	89		
Fear of Failure	33 (66.0)	17 (34.0)	50	0.6042	0.962 @
Inferiority Complex	30 (61.2)	19 (38.8)	49		
Others	20 (60.6)	13 (39.4)	33		
Total	193	122	315		

@ Denotes not significant

This study shows that the students, irrespective of their educational qualifications (undergraduate / postgraduate level), all have a similar kind of psychological factors as a reason for the dropouts.

Sub-hypothesis 1.9

There is no association between the students who studied in the different universities and the psychological factors as a reason for the dropouts.

As per Table 4.9 the P-value is greater than 0.05 levels; there is no association between the students who are studying in the different universities and the psychological factors as a reason for the dropouts from the distance education stream. Therefore, the null hypothesis is accepted.

Table 4.9

Chi-square Test for Association between University Studied and Psychological Factors

Psychological factors	*University studied*					
	Madras University	*Bharathi-dasan University*	*Madurai Kamaraj University*	*Total*	*Chi Square Value*	*P-Value*
Lack of Interest	38	30	26			
	(40.4)	(31.9)	(27.7)	94		
Lack of Memory	36	20	33			
	(40.4)	(22.5)	(37.1)	89		
Fear of Failure	16	21	13			
	(32.0)	(42.0)	(26.0)	50	14.554	0.068 @
Inferiority	27	12	10			
complex	(55.1)	(24.5)	(20.4)	49		
Others	9	14	10			
	(27.3)	(42.4)	(30.3)	33		
Total	126	97	92	315		

Note: The value within bracket refers to percentage, @ Denotes not significant

* Denotes significant at 0.05% level, ** Denotes significant at 0.01% level

This study brought to light that the students belonging to different universities had a similar kind of psychological factors as reasons for the dropouts.

Sub-hypothesis 1.10

There is no association between the employment status and the psychological factors as a reason for the dropouts.

As per Table 4.10, the P-value is greater than 0.05 levels; there is no association between the students' employment status and the psychological factors as a reason the for the dropouts from the distance education institution. Therefore, the null hypothesis is accepted.

Table 4.10

Chi-square Test for Association between Employment Status and Psychological Factors

Psychological factors	*Employment status*				
	Employed	*Unemployed*	*Total*	*Chi Square Value*	*P-Value*
Lack of Interest	58	36			
	(61.7)	(38.3)	94		
Lack of Memory	61	28			
	(68.5)	(31.5)	89		
Fear of Failure	34	16			
	(68.0)	(32.0)	50	1.365	0.850 @
Inferiority Complex	34	15			
	(69.4)	(30.6)	49		
Others	22	11			
	(66.7)	(33.3)	33		
Total	209	106	315		

@ Denotes not significant

It is observed that the employment status of the dropouts does not play a major role as a reason for the dropouts.

Sub-hypothesis 1.11

There is no association between the family's annual income and the psychological factors as a reason for the dropouts.

As per Table 4.11 the P-value is in association at 0.01 per cent level between the family's annual income and the psychological factors as a reason for the dropouts from the distance education institution. Therefore, the null hypothesis is rejected.

It is observed that the annual income of the family plays a major role as a reason for the dropout. The annual income is a major factor for the dropouts.

Table 4.11

Chi-square Test for Association between a Family's Annual income and psychological factors

Psychological factors	*Family's annual income (in rupees)*					
	Below 20,000	*20,000-30,000*	*Above 30,000*	*Total*	*Chi Square Value*	*P-Value*
Lack of Interest	16 (17.0)	38 (40.4)	40 (42.6)	94		
Lack of Memory	26 (29.2)	34 (38.2)	29 (32.6)	89		
Fear of Failure	14 (28.0)	7 (14.0)	29 (58.0)	50	20.856	0.007**
Inferiority Complex	8 (16.3)	15 (30.6)	26 (53.1)	49		
Others	4 (12.1)	15 (45.5)	14 (42.4)	33		
Total	68	109	138	315		

** Significant at 0.01 per cent level

Major Hypothesis 2

There will be no association between family-related factors and the personal attributions.

Sub-hypothesis 2.1

There is no association between the age group and the family-related factor as a reason for the dropout.

As per Table 4.12, the P-value is greater than 0.05 levels; there is no association between the age group and the family-related factors as a reason for the dropouts from the distance education institution.

Therefore, the null hypothesis is accepted. It is observed that the age group of the dropout did not play a vital role in association with the family-related factors as a reason for the dropouts.

Table 4.12

Chi-square Test for Association between Age Group and Family Related Factors

Family-related factors	*Age group*					
	18-22	*23-27*	*Above 27*	*Total*	*Chi Square Value*	*P-Value*
Children's education	2 (7.4)	10 (37.0)	15 (55.6)	27		
More Work in House	9 (16.1)	29 (51.8)	18 (32.1)	56		
Lack of Motivation in Family	15 (26.3)	26 (45.6)	16 (28.1)	57	12.567	0.127@
Financial Problems	18 (15.0)	56 (46.7)	46 (38.3)	120		
Others	7 (12.7)	32 (58.2)	16 (29.1)	55		
Total	51	153	111	315		

@ Denotes not significant

Table 4.13

Chi-square Test for Association between Sex and Family-related Factors

Family-related factors	*Sex*				
	Male	*Female*	*Total*	*Chi Square Value*	*P-Value*
Children's Education	7 (25.9)	20 (74.1)	27		
More Work in House	40 (71.4)	16 (28.6)	56		
Lack of Motivation in Family	33 (57.9)	24 (42.1)	57	20.736	0.000**
Financial Problems	83 (69.2)	37 (30.8)	120		
Others	37 (67.3)	18 (32.7)	55		
Total	169	146	315		

** Significant at 0.01 per cent level

Sub-hypothesis 2.2

There is no association between sex and family-related factors as a reason for the dropouts.

As per Table 4.13 the P-value is 0.01 per cent levels; there is an association between the sex and the family-related factors as a reason for the dropouts from the distance education institution.

Therefore, the null hypothesis is accepted. It is observed that the sex of the dropout plays a vital role in association with the family-related factors as a reason for the dropouts.

Sub-hypothesis 2.3

There is no association between marital status and the family-related factors as a reason for the dropouts.

Table 4.14

Chi-square test for Association between Marital Status and Family Related Factors

Family-related factors	*Marital status*				
	Married	*Unmarried*	*Total*	*Chi Square Value*	*P-Value*
Children's Education	25 (92.6)	2 (7.4)	27		
More Work in House	25 (44.6)	31 (55.4)	56		
Lack of Motivation in Family	22 (38.6)	35 (61.4)	57	26.833	0.000**
Financial Problems	59 (49.2)	61 (50.8)	120		
Others	20 (36.4)	35 (63.6)	55		
Total	151	164	315		

* * Significant at 0.01 per cent level

As per Table 4.14 the P-value is significant at 0.01 per cent levels; there is an association between the marital status and the family related factors as a reason for the dropouts from the distance education institution.

Therefore, the null hypothesis is rejected. It is observed that the marital status of the dropout plays a vital role in association with the family-related factors as a reason for the dropouts.

Sub-hypothesis 2.4

There is no association between the type of family and the family-related factors as a reason for the dropout.

As per Table 4.15 the P-value is significant at 0.01 per cent levels; there is an association between the type of family and the family-related factors as a reason for the dropouts from the distance education institution.

Table 4.15

Chi-square Test for Association between Type of Family and Family Related Factors

Family-related factors	*Type of family*				
	Nuclear	*Joint*	*Total*	*Chi Square Value*	*P-Value*
Children's Education	17 (63.0)	10 (37.0)	27		
More Work in House	19 (33.9)	37 (66.1)	56		
Lack of Motivation in Family	11 (19.3)	46 (80.7)	57	17.674	0.001**
Financial Problems	36 (30.0)	84 (70.0)	120		
Others	14 (25.5)	41 (74.5)	55		
Total	97	218	315		

* * Significant at 0.01 per cent level

Therefore, the null hypothesis is rejected. It is observed that the type of family of the dropouts plays a vital role in association with the family-related factors as a reason for the dropouts.

Sub-hypothesis 2.5

There is no association between religion and the family-related factors as a reason for the dropouts.

As per Table 4.16 the P-value is greater than 0.05 levels; there is no association between the religion and the family-related factors as a reason for the dropouts from the distance education institution.

Therefore, the null hypothesis is accepted. It is observed that the religion of the dropouts did not play a vital role in association with the family-related factors as a reason for the dropouts.

Sub-hypothesis 2.6

There is no association between community and the family-related factors as a reason for the dropouts.

Table 4.16: Chi-square Test for association between Religion and Family-related Factors

Psychological factors	*Religion*					
	Hindu	*Muslim*	*Christian*	*Total*	*Chi Square Value*	*P-Value*
Children's Education	15 (55.6)	9 (33.3)	3 (11.1)	27		
More Work in House	36 (64.3)	9 (16.1)	11 (19.6)	56		
Lack of Motivation in Family	28 (49.1)	20 (35.1)	9 (15.8)	57	11.753	0.162@
Financial Problems	77 (64.2)	22 (18.3)	21 (17.5)	120		
Others	30 (69.1)	11 (20.0)	6 (10.9)	55		
Total	194	71	50	315		

@ Denotes not significant

Table 4.17: Chi-square Test for Association between Communities and Family-related Factors

Family-related factors	*Community*						
	B.C	*M.B.C*	*SC/ST*	*OC*	*Total*	*Chi Square Value*	*P - Value*
Children's Education	14 (51.9)	5 (18.5)	5 (18.5)	3 (11.1)	27		
More Work in house	22 (39.3)	20 (35.7)	10 (17.9)	4 (7.1)	56		
Lack of Motivation in Family	34 (59.6)	5 (8.8)	11 (19.3)	7 (12 3)	57	25.764	0.011*
Economic Problems	58 (48.3)	25 (20.8)	20 (23.3)	9 (7.5)	120		
Others	19 (34.5)	24 (43.6)	7 (12.7)	5 (9.1)	55		
Total	147	79	61	28	315		

* Significant at 0.05 per cent level

As per Table 4.17, the P-value is significant at 0.05 per cent levels; there is an association between the religion of the dropouts and the family-related factors as a reason for the dropouts from the distance education institution.

Therefore, the null hypothesis is rejected and the alternative hypothesis is accepted. The community of the students and the family-related factors does not influence as a reason for the dropouts.

Sub-hypothesis 2.7

There is no association between the place of birth and the family-related factors as a reason for the dropouts.

As per Table 4.18, the P-value is greater than 0.05 levels; there is an association between the place of birth and the family-related factors as a reason for the dropouts from the distance education institution.

Therefore, the null hypothesis is rejected. It is observed that the place of birth of the dropouts plays a vital role in association with the family related factors as a reason for the dropouts.

Table 4.18

Chi-square Test for Association between Places of Birth and Family-related Factors

Family-related factors	*Place of birth*				
	Urban	*Rural*	*Total*	*Chi Square Value*	*P-Value*
Children's Education	13 (48.1)	14 (51.9)	27		
More Work in House	28 (50.0)	28 (50.0)	56		
Lack of Motivation in Family	37 (64.9)	20 (35.1)	57	9.566	0.048*
Financial Problems	55 (45.8)	65 (54.2)	120		
Others	36 (65.5)	19 (34.5)	55		
Total	169	146	315		

* Significant at 0.05 per cent level

Table 4.19

Chi-square Test for Association between Educational Qualifications and Family-related Factors

Family-related factors	*Educational qualifications*				
	U.G	*P.G*	*Total*	*Chi Square Value*	*P-Value*
Children's Education	18 (66.7)	9 (33.3)	27		
More Work in House	37 (66.1)	19 (33.9)	56		
Lack of Motivation in Family	30 (52.6)	27 (47.4)	57	9.731	0.045*
Financial Problems	82 (68.3)	38 (31.7)	120		
Others	26 (47.3)	29 (52.7)	55		
Total	193	122	315		

* Significant at 0.05 per cent level

Sub-hypothesis 2.8

There is no association between educational qualifications and the family-related factors as a reason for the dropouts.

As per Table 4.19 the P-value is 0.05 per cent levels; there is an association between the educational qualifications and the family-related factors as a reason for the dropouts from the distance education institution. Therefore, the null hypothesis is rejected.

It is observed that the educational qualification of the dropout plays a vital role in association with the family-related factors as a reason for the dropouts.

Sub hypothesis 2.9

There is no association between the university studied and the family-related factors as reasons for the dropouts.

Table 4.20

Chi-square test for Association between universities studied and family related factors

Family-related factors	*University studied*					
	Madras University	*Bharathi-dasan University*	*Madurai Kamaraj University*	*Total*	*Chi Square Value*	*P-Value*
Children's Education	11 (40.7)	5 (18.5)	11 (40.7)	27		
More Work in House	24 (42.9)	17 (30.4)	15 (26.8)	56		
Lack of Motivation in Family	23 (40.4)	18 (31.6)	16 (28.1)	57	5.199	0.736 @
Financial Problems	51 (42.5)	37 (30.8)	32 (26.7)	120		
Others	17 (30.9)	20 (36.4)	18 (32.7)	55		
Total	126	97	92	315		

@ Denotes not significant

As per Table 4.20, the P-value is greater than 0.05 levels; there is no association between the university studied and the family- related factors as a reason for the dropouts from the distance education institution. Therefore, the null hypothesis is accepted.

The family-related factors and the students studying in different universities do not influence as a major factor for the dropouts in the distance education stream.

Sub-hypothesis 2.10

There is no association between the employment status and the family-related factors as a reason for the dropouts.

Table 4.21

Chi-square Test for Association between Employment Status and Family-related Factors

Family-related factors	*Employment status*				
	Employed	*Unemployed*	*Total*	*Chi Square Value*	*P-Value*
Children's Education	11 (40.7)	16 (59.3)	27		
More Work in House	40 (71.4)	16 (28.6)	56		
Lack of Motivation in Family	37 (64.9)	20 (35.1)	57	9.367	0.052@
Financial Problems	84 (70.0)	36 (30.0)	120		
Others	37 (67.3)	18 (32.7)	55		
Total	209	106	315		

@ Denotes not significant

As per Table 4.21, the P-value is greater than 0.05 levels; there is no association between the employment status and the family-related factors as a reason for the dropouts from the distance education institution.

Therefore, the null hypothesis is accepted. It is observed that the employment status of the dropout did not play a vital role in association with the family-related factors as a reason for the dropouts.

Sub-hypothesis 2.11

There is no association between the family's annual income and the family-related factors as a reason for the dropouts.

Table 4.22

Chi-square Test for Association between Family Annual Income and Family-related Factors

Family-related factors	*Family's Annual Income (in Rupees)*					
	Below 20,000	*20,000-30,000*	*Above 30,000*	*Total*	*Chi Square Value*	*P-Value*
Children's Education	8 (29.6)	9 (33.3)	10 (37.0)	27		
More Work in House	10 (17.9)	31 (55.4)	15 (26.8)	56		
Lack of Motivation in Family	8 (14.0)	24 (42.1)	25 (43.9)	57	55.286	0.000**
Financial Problems	37 (30.80)	14 (11.7)	69 (57.5)	120		
Others	50 (9.1)	31 (56.4)	19 (34.5)	55		
Total	68	109	138	315		

** Significant at 0.01 per cent level

As per Table 4.22 the P-value is significant at 0.01 levels; there is an association between the family's annual income and the family-related factors as a reason for the dropouts from the distance education institution.

Therefore, the null hypothesis is rejected. It is observed that the annual family income of the dropout plays a vital role in association with the family-related factors as a reason for the dropouts.

Major Hypothesis 3

There will be no association between social-related factors and the personal attributions.

Sub-hypothesis 3.1

There is no association between age group and social-related factors as a reason for the dropouts.

Table 4.23

Chi-square Test for Association between Age Group and Social-related Factors

Social factors	*Age group*					
	18-22	*23-27*	*Above 27*	*Total*	*Chi Square Value*	*P-Value*
Religious cause	10	38	26			
	(13.5)	(51.4)	(35.1)	74		
Education not	18	42	19	79		
required for Women	(22.8)	(53.2)	(24.1)			
Marital status	5	26	32			
	(7.9)	(41.3)	(50.8)	63	16.845	0.031*
Opposition by the	11	35	19			
relatives	(16.9)	(53.8)	(29.2)	65		
Others	7	12	15			
	(20.6)	(35.3)	(44.1)	34		
Total	51	153	111	315		

@ Significant at 0.05 per cent level

As per Table 4.23, the P-value is significant at 0.05 per cent level; there is an association between the age group of the dropouts and the social-related factors as a reason for the dropouts from the distance education institution.

Therefore, the null hypothesis is rejected. It is observed that the age group of the dropouts plays a positive role in association with the social-related factors as a reason for the dropouts.

Sub-hypothesis 3.2

There is no association between sex and social-related factors as a reason for the dropout.

As per the Table 4.24 the P-value is not significant; there is no association between the sex and the social factors as a reason for the dropouts from the distance education institution.

Therefore, the null hypothesis is accepted. It was observed that the sex of the dropouts does not play any role in association with the social-related factors as a reason for the dropouts.

Table 4.24

Chi-square Test for Association between Sex and Social-related Factors

	Sex				
Social factors	*Male*	*Female*	*Total*	*Chi Square Value*	*P-Value*
Religious Cause	50 (67.6)	24 (32.4)	74		
Education not Required for Women	48 (60.8)	31 (39.2)	79		
Marital Status	36 (57.1)	27 (42.9)	63	2.396	0.663@
Opposition by the Relatives	44 (67.7)	21 (32.3)	65		
Others	22 (64.7)	12 (35.3)	34		
Total	200	115	315		

@ Denotes not significant

Sub-hypothesis 3.3

There is no association between marital status and the social related factors as a reason for dropout.

As per Table 4.25, the P-value is significant at 0.01 per cent level; there is an association between the marital status of the dropouts and the social-related factors as a reason for the dropouts from the distance education institution.

Therefore, the null hypothesis is rejected. It is observed that the marital status of the dropouts plays a vital role in association with the social-related factors as a reason for the dropouts.

Sub-hypothesis 3.4

There is no association between the types of family and the social-related factors as a reason for the dropouts.

Table 4.25

Chi-square Test for Association between Marital Status and Social-Related Factors

Social factors	*Marital status*				
	Married	*Unmarried*	*Total*	*Chi Square Value*	*P-Value*
Religious Cause	25	49	74		
	(33.8)	(66.2)			
Education not	30	49			
Required for Women	(38.0)	(62.0)	79		
Marital Status	62	1			
	(98.4)	(1.6)	63	81.229	0.000**
Opposition by the	24	41			
Relatives	(36.9)	(63.1)	65		
Others	10	24			
	(29.2)	(70.6)	34		
Total	151	164	315		

** Significant at 0.01 per cent level

As per Table 4.26, P-value is significant at 0.01 per cent level; there is an association between the type of family and the social related factors as a reason for the dropouts from the distance education institution.

Table 4.26

Chi-square Test for Association between Type of Family and Social-related Factors

	Type of family				
Social factors	*Nuclear*	*Joint*	*Total*	*Chi Square Value*	*P-Value*
Religious Cause	18	56			
	(24.3)	(75.7)	74		
Education not	23	56			
Required for Women	(29.1)	(70.9)	79		
Marital Status	34	29			
	(54.0)	(46.0)	63	23.341	0.000**
Opposition by the	11	54			
Relatives	(16.9)	(83.1)	65		
Others	11	23			
	(32.4)	(67.6)	34		
Total	97	218	315		

** Significant at 0.01 per cent level

Therefore, the null hypothesis is rejected. It is observed that the type of family of the dropouts and the related social factors play a proximate role as a reason for the dropouts in distance education stream.

Sub-hypothesis 3.5

There is no association between religion and the social-related factors as a reason for the dropouts.

As per Table 4.27, the P-value is not significant; there is no association between the religion and the social-related factors as a reason for the dropouts from the distance education institution.

Therefore, the null hypothesis is accepted. It is observed that the religion of the dropout did not play any role in association with the social-related factors as a reason for the dropouts.

Table 4.27

Chi-square Test for Association between Religion and Social-related Factors

Social factors	*Religion*					
	Hindu	*Muslim*	*Christian*	*Total*	*Chi Square Value*	*P-Value*
Religious cause	42 (56.8)	15 (20.3)	17 (23.0)	74		
Education not required for Women	44 (55.7)	22 (27.8)	13 (16.5)	79		
Marital status	42 (66.7)	15 (23.8)	6 (9.5)	63	9.170	0.328@
Opposition by the relatives	46 (70.8)	12 (18.5)	7 (10.8)	65		
Others	20 (58.8)	7 (20.6)	7 (20.6)	34		
Total	194	71	50	315		

@ Denotes not significant

Sub-hypothesis 3.6

There is no association between community and the social related factors as a reason for the dropouts.

As per Table 4.28, the P-value is not significant; there is no association between the community of the dropouts and the social-related factors as a reason for dropouts from the distance education institution.

Therefore, the null hypothesis is accepted. It is observed that the community of the dropouts did not play any role in association with the social-related factors as a reason for the dropouts.

Table 4.28

Chi-square test for Association between Community and Social-related Factors

Social factors	*Community*						
	B.C	*M.B.C*	*SC/ST*	*OC*	*Total*	*Chi Square Value*	*P - Value*
Religious Cause	27 (36.5)	24 (32.4)	15 (20.3)	8 (10.8)	74		
Education not Required for Women	39 (49.4)	22 (27.8)	11 (13.9)	7 (8.9)	79		
Marital Status	30 (47.6)	10 (15.9)	17 (27.0)	6 (9.5)	63	11.742	0.466@
Opposition by the Relatives	34 (52.3)	16 (24.6)	12 (18.5)	3 (4.6)	65		
Others	17 (50.0)	7 (20.6)	6 (17.6)	4 (11.8)	34		
Total	147	79	61	28	315		

@ Denotes not significant

***Sub-hypothesis** 3.7*

There is no association between place of birth and the social factors as a reason for dropout.

As per Table 4.29, the P-value is not significant; there is no association between the place of birth of the dropouts and the social-related factors as a reason for the dropouts from the distance education institution.

Therefore, the null hypothesis is accepted. It is observed that place of birth of the dropouts did not play any role in association with the social-related factors as a reason for the dropouts.

Table 4.29

Chi-square Test for Association between Place of Birth and Social-related Factors

Social factors	*Place of Birth*				
	Urban	*Rural*	*Total*	*Chi Square Value*	*P-Value*
Religious Cause	42	32			
	(56.8)	(43.2)	74		
Education not	41	38			
Required for Women	(51.9)	(48.1)	79		
Marital Status	29	34			
	(46.0)	(54.0)	63	3.527	0.473@
Opposition by the	35	30			
Relatives	(53.8)	(46.2)	65		
Others	22	12			
	(64.7)	(35.3)	34		
Total	169	146	315		

@ Denotes not significant

***Sub-hypothesis** 3.8*

There is no association between educational qualifications and social-related factors as a reason for the dropout.

As per Table 4.30, the P-value is not significant; there is no association between the educational qualifications and the social factors as a reason for the dropouts from the distance education institution.

Therefore, the null hypothesis is accepted. It is observed that the educational qualification of the dropouts did not play any role in association with the social-related factors as a reason for the dropouts.

Table 4.30

Chi-square Test for Association between Educational Qualifications and Social-related Factors

Social factors	*Educational qualifications*				
	U.G	*P.G*	*Total*	*Chi Square Value*	*P-Value*
Religious Cause	42	32	74		
	(56.8)	(43.2)			
Education not Required	48	31			
for Women	(60.8)	(39.2)	79		
Marital Status	36	27			
	(57.1)	(42.9)	63		
Opposition by the	48	17		5.844	0.211@
Relatives	(73.8)	(26.2)	65		
Others	19	15			
	(55.9)	(44.1)	34		
Total	193	122	315		

@ Denotes not significant

Sub-hypothesis 3.9

There is no association between university studied and the social related factors as a reason for dropouts.

As per Table 4.31, the P-value is not significant; there is no association between the university studied and the social factors as a reason for the dropouts from the distance education institution.

Therefore, the null hypothesis is accepted. It is observed that the university in which the dropouts studied did not play any role in association with the social-related factors as a reason for the dropouts.

Table 4.31

Chi-square Test for Association between Universities Studied and Social-related Factors

Social factors	*University studied*					
	Madras University	*Bharathi-dasan University*	*Madurai Kamaraj University*	*Total*	*Chi Square Value*	*P-Value*
Religious Cause	39	12	23			
	(52.7)	(16.2)	(31.1)	74		
Education not	30	28	21			
Required for Women	(38.0)	(35.4)	(26.6)	79		
Marital Status	22	20	21			
	(34.9)	(31.7)	(33.3)	63	13.405	0.098@
Opposition	23	22	20			
by the Relatives	(35.4)	(33.8)	(30.8)	65		
Others	12	15	7			
	(35.3)	(44.1)	(20.6)	34		
Total	126	97	92	315		

@ Denotes not significant

Sub-hypothesis 3.10

There is no association between employment status and social-related factors as a reason for the dropouts.

As per Table 4.32, the P-value is not significant; there is no association between the employment status and the employment-related factors as a reason for the dropouts from the distance education institution.

Therefore, the null hypothesis is accepted. It is observed that the employment status of the dropouts did not play any role in association with the social-related factors as a reason for the dropouts.

Table 4.32

Chi-square test for Association between Employment Status and Social-related Factors

Social factors	*Employment status*				
	Employed	*Unemployed*	*Total*	*Chi Square Value*	*P-Value*
Religious Cause	51 (68.9)	23 (31.1)	74		
Education not Required for Women	57 (72.2)	22 (27.8)	79		
Marital Status	40 (63.5)	23 (36.5)	63		
Opposition by the Relatives	40 (61.5)	25 (38.5)	65	2.634	0.630@
Others	21 (61.8)	13 (38.2)	34		
Total	209	106	315		

@ Denotes not significant

Sub-hypothesis 3.11

There is no association between the university studied and the social-related factors as a reason for the dropouts.

As per Table 4.33, the P-value is not significant; there is no association between the family annual income of the dropouts and the social related factors as a reason for the dropouts from the distance education institution.

Therefore, the null hypothesis is accepted. It is observed that the family annual income of the dropouts did not play any role in association with the social-related factors as a reason for the dropout.

Major-Hypothesis 4

There will be no association between health-related factors and personal attributions.

Table 4.33

Chi-square Test for Association between Family's Annual Income and Social-related Factors

Social factors	*Family's annual income (in rupees)*					
	Below 20,000	*20,000-30,000*	*Above 30,000*	*Total*	*Chi Square Value*	*P-Value*
Religious Cause	16	26	32			
	(21.6)	(35.1)	(43.2)	74		
Education not	11	27	41			
Required for Women	(13.9)	(34.2)	(51.9)	79		
Marital Status	19	17	27			
	(30.2)	(27.0)	(42.9)	63	9.770	0.281@
Opposition by	14	23	28			
the Relatives	(21.5)	(35.4)	(43.1)	65		
Others	8	16	10			
	(23.5)	(47.1)	(29.4)	34		
Total	68	109	138	15		

@ Denotes not significant

***Sub-hypothesis* 4.1**

There is no association between age group and health-related factors as a reason for the dropouts.

As per Table 4.34, the P-value is greater than 0.05 levels; there is no association between the age group of the dropouts and the health-related factors as a reason for the dropouts from the distance education institution.

Therefore, the null hypothesis is accepted. It is observed that the age group of the dropouts does not play a vital role in association with the health-related factors as a reason for the dropouts.

***Sub-hypothesis* 4.2**

There is no association between sex and the health-related factors as a reason for the dropouts.

Table 4.34

Chi-square Test for Association between Age Group and Health-related Factors

Health-related factors	*Age group*					
	18-22	*23-27*	*Above 27*	*Total*	*Chi Square Value*	*P-Value*
Disability	3 (9.4)	17 (53.1)	12 (37.5)	32		
Chronic Illness	24 (18.0)	61 (45.9)	48 (36.1)	133		
Ill Health of Family members	17 (15.2)	59 (52.7)	36 (32.1)	112	3.013	0.807@
Others	7 (18.4)	16 (42.1)	15 (39.5)	38		
Total	51	153	111	315		

@ Denotes not significant

Table 4.35

Chi-square Test for Association between Sex and Health-related Factors

Health-related factors	*Sex*				
	Male	*Female*	*Total*	*Chi Square Value*	*P-Value*
Disability	21 (65.6)	11 (34.4)	32		
Chronic Illness	88 (66.2)	45 (33.8)	133		
Ill health of Family Members	69 (61.6)	43 (38.4)	112	1.158	0.763@
Others	22 (57.9)	16 (42.1)	38		
Total	200	115	315		

@ Denotes not significant

As per Table 4.35, the P-value is greater than 0.05 levels; there is no association between the sex of the dropouts and their health-related factors as a reason for the dropouts from the distance education institution.

Therefore, the null hypothesis is accepted. It is observed that the sex of the dropouts does not play a vital role in association with the health-related factors as a reason for the dropouts.

Sub-hypothesis – 4.3

There is no association between marital status and the health related factors as a reason for dropout.

As per Table 4.36, the P-value is greater than 0.05 levels; there is no association between the marital status of the dropouts and the health-related factors as a reason for the dropouts from the distance education institution.

Therefore, the null hypothesis is accepted. It is observed that the marital status of the dropouts does not influence in association with the health-related factors as a reason for the dropouts.

Table 4.36

Chi-square Test for Association between Marital Status and Health-related Factors

Health-related Factors	*Marital status*				
	Married	*Unmarried*	*Total*	*Chi Square Value*	*P-Value*
Disability	18 (56.3)	14 (43.8)	32		
Chronic Illness	63 (47.4)	70 (52.6)	133		
Ill health of Family Members	49 (43.8)	63 (56.3)	112	2.507	0.473@
Others	21 (55.3)	17 (44.7)	38		
Total	151	164	315		

@ Denotes not significant

Table 4.37

Chi-square Test for Association between the Type of Family and Health-related Factors

Health-related Factors	*Type of family*				
	Nuclear	*Joint*	*Total*	*Chi Square Value*	*P-Value*
Disability	9	23	32		
	(28.1)	(71.9)			
Chronic Illness	43	90	133		
	(32.3)	(67.7)			
Ill Health of	32	80			
Family Members	(28.6)	(71.4)	112	0.722	0.867@
Others	13	25			
	(34.2)	(65.8)	38		
Total	97	218	315		

@ Denotes not significant

***Sub-hypothesis* 4.4**

There is no association between the type of family and the health-related factors as a reason for the dropouts.

As per Table 4.37, the P-value is greater than 0.05 levels; there is no association between the type of family of the dropouts and the health-related factors as a reason for the dropouts from the distance education institution.

Therefore, the null hypothesis is accepted. It is observed that the type of family of the dropouts does not influence in association with the health-related factors as a reason for the dropouts.

***Sub-hypothesis* 4.5**

There is no association between religion and health related factors as a reason for the dropouts.

Table 4.38

Chi-square Test for Association between Religion and Health-related Factors

Health-related factors	*Religion*					
	Hindu	*Muslim*	*Christian*	*Total*	*Chi Square Value*	*P-Value*
Disability	18 (56.3)	9 (28.1)	5 (15.6)	32		
Chronic Illness	84 (63.2)	32 (24.1)	17 (12.8)	133		
Ill Health of Family Members	68 (60.7)	23 (20.5)	21 (18.8)	112	2.836	0.829@
Others	24 (63.2)	7 (18.4)	7 (18.4)	38		
Total	194	71	50	315		

@ Denotes not significant

As per Table 4.38, the P-value is greater than 0.05 levels; there is no association between the religion of the dropouts and the health-related factors as a reason for the dropouts from the distance education institution.

Therefore, the null hypothesis is accepted. It is observed that the religion of the dropout does not play a vital role in association with the health-related factors as a reason for the dropouts.

Sub-hypothesis 4.6

There is no association between community and health-related factors as a reason for the dropouts.

As per Table 4.39, the P-value is greater than 0.05 levels; there is no association between the community of the dropouts and the health-related factors as a reason for the dropouts from the distance education institution.

Table 4.39

Chi-square Test for Association between Community and Health-related Factors

Health-related factors	*Community*						
	B.C	*M.B.C*	*SC/ST*	*OC*	*Total*	*Chi Square Value*	*P - Value*
Disability	16 (50.0)	6 (18.8)	6 (18.8)	4 (12.5)	32		
Chronic Illness	63 (47.4)	41 (30.8)	18 (13.5)	11 (8.3)	133		
Ill Health of Family Members	50 (44.6)	26 (23.2)	26 (23.2)	10 (8.9)	112	9.488	0.393@
Others	18 (47.4)	6 (15.8)	11 (28.9	3 (7.9)	38		
Total	147	79	61	28	315		

@ Denotes not significant

Therefore, the null hypothesis is accepted. It is observed that the community of the dropouts does not influence in association with the health-related factors as a reason for the dropouts.

***Sub-hypothesis* 4.7**

There is no association between the place of birth and health related factors as a reason for the dropouts.

As per Table 4.40 the P-value is greater than 0.05 levels; there is no association between the place of birth of the dropouts and the health-related factors as a reason for dropouts from the distance education institution.

Therefore, the null hypothesis is accepted. It is observed that the place of birth of the dropout does not influence in association with the health-related factors as a reason for the dropout.

Table 4.40

Chi-square Test for Association between Place of Birth and Health-related Factors

Health-related factor	*Place of birth*				
	Urban	*Rural*	*Total*	*Chi Square Value*	*P-Value*
Disability	21	11			
	(65.6)	(34.4)	32		
Chronic Illness	78	55			
	(58.6)	(41.4)	133		
Ill Health of Family	51	61			
Members	(45.5)	(54.5)	112	6.349	0.095@
Others	19	19	38		
	(50.0)	(50.0)			
Total	169	146	315		

@ Denotes not significant

Table 4.41

Chi-square Test for Association between Educational Qualifications and Health-related Factors

Health-related factors	*Educational qualifications*				
	U.G	*P.G*	*Total*	*Chi Square Value*	*P-Value*
Disability	20	12			
	(62.5)	(37.5)	32		
Chronic Illness	81	52	133		
	(60.9)	(39.1)			
Ill Health of Family	65	47			
Members	(58.0)	(42.0)	112	2.054	0.561@
Others	27	11			
	(71.1)	(28.9)	38		
Total	193	122	315		

@ Denotes not significant

Sub-hypothesis 4.8

There is no association between educational qualifications and the health-related factors as a reason for the dropouts.

As per Table 4.41, the P-value is greater than 0.05 levels; there is no association between the educational qualifications of the dropouts and the health-related factors as a reason for the dropouts from the distance education institution.

Therefore, the null hypothesis is accepted. It is observed that the educational qualifications of the dropouts do not influence in association with the health-related factors as a reason for the dropouts.

Sub-hypothesis 4.9

There is no association between the university studied and health-related factors as a reason for dropouts.

Table 4.42

Chi-square Test for Association between University Studied and Health-related Factors

Health-related factors	*University studied*					
	Madras University	*Bharathi-dasan University*	*Madurai Kamaraj University*	*Total*	*Chi Square Value*	*P-Value*
Disability	18 (56.3)	0 (00.0)	14 (43.8)	32		
Chronic illness	43 (32.3)	51 (38.3)	39 (29.3)	133		
Ill Health of Family Members	46 (41.1)	39 (34.8)	27 (24.1)	112	23.235	0.000**
Others	19 (50.0)	7 (18.4)	12 (31.6)	38		
Total	126	97	92	315		

* * Significant at 0.01 per cent level

As per Table 4.42, the P-value is significant at 0.01 per cent level; there is an association between the university studied and the health-related factors as a reason for the dropouts from the distance education institution.

Therefore, the null hypothesis is rejected. It is observed that the university in which the dropouts studied plays a major role in association with the health-related factors as a reason for the dropouts.

Sub-hypothesis 4.10

There is no association between the employment status and health-related factors as a reason for dropout.

As per Table 4.43, the P-value is greater than 0.05 levels; there is no association between the employment status of the dropouts and the health-related factors as a reason for the dropouts from the distance education institution.

Therefore, the null hypothesis is accepted. It is observed that the employment of the dropouts does not influence in association with the health-related factors as a reason for the dropouts.

Sub-hypothesis 4.11

There is no association between the family's annual income and the health-related factors as a reason for the dropouts.

Table 4.43

Chi-square Test for Association between Employment Status and Health-related Factors

Health-related factors	*Employment status*				
	Employed	*Unemployed*	*Total*	*Chi Square Value*	*P-Value*
Disability	24 (75.0)	8 (25.0)	32		
Chronic Illness	86 (64.7)	47 (35.3)	133		
Ill Health of Family Members	75 (67.0)	37 (33.0)	112	1.434	0.697@
Others	24 (63.2)	14 (36.8)	38		
Total	209	106	315		

@ Denotes not significant

Table 4.44

Chi-square Test for Association between Family's Annual Income and Health-related Factors

Health related factors	*Family's annual income (in rupees)*					
	Below 20,000	*20,000-30,000*	*Above 30,000*	*Total*	*Chi Square Value*	*P-Value*
Disability	8	12	12	32		
	(25.0)	(37.5)	(37.5)			
Chronic Illness	28	43	62	133		
	(21.1)	(32.3)	(46.6)			
Ill Health of	25	42	45	112	2.242	0.896@
Family Members	(22.3)	(37.5)	(40.2)			
Others	7	12	19	38		
	(18.4)	(31.6)	(50.0)			
Total	68	109	138	315		

@ Denotes not significant

As per Table 4.44, the P-value is greater than 0.05 levels; there is no association between the family's annual income of the dropouts and the health-related factors as a reason for the dropouts from the distance education institution.

Therefore, the null hypothesis is accepted. It is observed that the family's annual income of the dropouts did not play a vital role in association with the health-related factors as a reason for the dropouts.

Major Hypothesis 5

There will be no association between educational-related factors and personal attributions.

Sub-hypothesis 5.1

There is no association between the age of dropouts and the education-related factors as a reason for the dropouts.

Table 4.45

Chi-square Test for Association between Age Group and Educational Factors

Educational factors	*Age Group* 18 - 22	23 - 27	Above 27	Total	Chi Square Value	P - Value
Hard Syllabus	10	29	22	61		
	(16.4)	(47.5)	(36.1)			
Lack of Library	4	13	10	27		
	(14.8)	(48.1)	(37.0)			
Less Memory	10	29	4	43		
	(23.3)	(67.4)	(9.3)			
Less Information	3	13	14	30		
	(10.0)	(43.3)	(46.7)		21.189	0.047*
No Clear Idea	6	24	20	50		
	(12.0)	(48.0)	(40.0)			
Unemployability	11	37	34	82		
	(13.4)	(45.0)	(41.5)			
Others	7	8	7	22		
	(31.8)	(36.4)	(31.8)			
Total	51	153	111	315		

* Significant at 0.05 per cent level

As per Table 4.45, the P-value is significant at 0.05 per cent level. The age group of dropouts and the educational-related factors play a role in dropping out from the distance education institution. Therefore, the null hypothesis is rejected.

It is observed that the students' age group has different kinds of educational-related factors as a reason for the dropouts.

Sub-hypothesis 5.2

There is no association between gender of dropouts and the educational related factors as a reason for dropout.

As per Table 4.46 the P-value is greater than 0.05 levels; there is no association between the gender of student dropouts and the educational-related factors as a reason for dropouts from the distance education institution. Therefore, the null hypothesis is accepted.

Table 4.46

Chi-square Test for Association between Sex and Educational Factor

Educational factors	*Sex*				
	Male	*Female*	*Total*	*Chi Square Value*	*P-Value*
Hard Syllabus	39 (63.9)	22 (36.1)	61		
Lack of Library	14 (51.9)	13 (48.1)	27		
Less Memory	24 (55.8)	19 (44.2)	43		
Less Information	22 (73.4)	8 (26.7)	30	5.074	0.534 @
No Clear Idea	35 (70.0)	15 (30.0)	50		
Unemployability	53 (64.6)	29 (35.4)	82		
Others	13 (59.1)	9 (40.9)	22		
Total	200	115	315		

@ Denotes not significant

It is observed that both male and female students were having a similar kind of educational-related factors as a reason for the dropouts.

Sub-hypothesis 5.3

There is no association between the marital status of the dropouts and the educational-related factors as a reason for the dropouts.

As per Table 4.47 the P-value is in association between the marital status and the educational-related factors as a reason for the dropouts from the distance education system. Therefore, the null hypothesis is rejected.

The students' marital status plays a major role in association with the educational-related factors as a reason for the dropouts.

Table 4.47

Chi-square Test for Association between Marital Status and Educational Factor

Educational factors	*Marital status*				
	Married	*Unmarried*	*Total*	*Chi Square Value*	*P-Value*
Hard Syllabus	30 (49.2)	31 (50.8)	61		
Lack of Library	16 (59.3)	11 (40.7)	27		
Less Memory	13 (30.2)	30 (69.8)	43		
Less Information	10 (33.3)	20 (66.7)	30	15.895	0.014*
No Clear Idea	29 (58.0)	21 (42.0)	50		
Unemployability	46 (56.1)	36 (43.9)	82		
Others	7 (31.8)	15 (68.2)	22		
Total	151	164	315		

* Significant at 0.05 per cent level

Sub-hypothesis 5.4

There is no association between the type of family and the educational-related factors as a reason for the dropout.

As per Table 4.48 the P-value is greater than 0.05 levels; there is no association between the type of family of the student and the educational-related factors as a reason for dropouts from the distance education institution. Therefore, the null hypothesis is accepted.

Table 4.48

Chi-square Test for Association between the Type of Family and Educational Factors

	Type of family				
Educational factors	*Nuclear*	*Joint*	*Total*	*Chi Square Value*	*P-Value*
Hard Syllabus	22	39	61		
	(36.1)	(63.9)			
Lack of Library	8	19	27		
	(29.6)	(70.4)			
Less Memory	6	37	43		
	(14.0)	(86.0)			
Less Information	11	19	30	9.578	0.143@
	(36.7)	(63.3)			
No Clear Idea	13	37	50		
	(26.0)	(74.0)			
Unemployability	31	51	82		
	(37.8)	(62.2)			
Others	6	16	22		
	(27.3)	(72.7)			
Total	97	218	315		

@ Denotes not significant

It is observed that the family type and related educational factors do not influence as a factor for the dropouts.

Sub-hypothesis 5.5

There is no association between the religion of the dropouts and the education-related factors as a reason for the dropouts.

As per Table 4.49 the P-value is greater than 0.05 levels; there is no association between the religion of the student and the educational-related factors as a reason for the dropouts from the distance education institution. Therefore, the null hypothesis is accepted.

There is no association between religion and educational-related factors as a reason for the dropouts.

Table 4.49

Chi-square Test for Association between Religion of Dropout and Educational Factor

Educational factors	*Religion*					
	Hindu	*Muslim*	*Christian*	*Total*	*Chi Square Value*	*P-Value*
Hard Syllabus	47 (77.0)	8 (13.1)	6 (9.8)	61		
Lack of Library	15 (55.6)	8 (29.6)	4 (14.8)	27		
Less Memory	30 (69.8)	9 (20.9)	4 (9.3)	43		
Less Information	14 (46.7)	11 (36.7)	5 (16.7)	30	18.800	0.093@
No Clear Idea	27 (54.0)	11 (22.0)	12 (24.0)	50		
Unemployability	45 (54.9)	22 (26.8)	15 (18.3)	82		
Others	16 (72.7)	2 (9.1)	4 (18.2)	22		
Total	194	71	50	315		

@ Denotes not significant

Sub-hypothesis 5.6

There is no association between the communities of dropouts and the education-related factors as a reason for the dropouts.

As per Table 4.50 the P-value is greater than 0.05 levels; there is no association between the community of the students and the educational-related factors as a reason for the dropouts from the distance education institution. Therefore, the null hypothesis is accepted.

Table 4.50

Chi-square Test for Association between Communities and Educational Factor

	Community						
Educational factors	*B.C*	*M.B.C*	*SC/ST*	*OC*	*Total*	*Chi Square Value*	*P - Value*
Hard Syllabus	26 (42.6)	22 (36.1)	8 (13.1)	5 (8.2)	61		
Lack of Library	12 (44.4)	5 (18.5)	7 (25.9)	3 (11.1)	27		
Less Memory	23 (53.5)	10 (23.3)	7 (16.3)	3 (7.0)	43		
Less Information	16 (53.3)	5 (16.7)	4 (13.3)	5 (16.7)	30	13.540	0.758@
No Clear Idea	25 (50.0)	9 (18.0)	12 (24.0)	4 (8.0)	50		
Unemploy-ability	36 (43.9)	21 (25.6)	19 (23.2)	6 (7.3)	82		
Others	9 (40.9)	7 (31.8)	4 (18.2)	2 (9.1)	22		
Total	147	79	61	28	315		

@ Denotes not significant

It is observed that the community of the dropouts does not play a vital role in educational-related factors as a reason for the dropouts.

Sub-hypothesis 5.7

There is no association between the place of birth of dropouts and educational-related factors as a reason for the dropouts.

As per Table 4.51 the P-value is greater than 0.05 levels; there is no association between the place of birth of the students and the educational-related factors as a reason for the dropouts from the distance education institution. Therefore, the null hypothesis is accepted.

It was observed that the place of birth of the dropouts has no influence on educational-related factors as a reason for the dropouts.

Table 4.51

Chi-square Test for Association between Place of Birth and Educational Factors

Educational factors	*Place of birth*				
	Urban	*Rural*	*Total*	*Chi Square Value*	*P-Value*
Hard Syllabus	33 (54.1)	28 (45.9)	61		
Lack of Library	11 (40.7)	16 (59.3)	27		
Less Memory	20 (46.5)	23 (53.5)	43		
Less Information	24 (80.0)	6 (20.0)	30	11.650	0.070@
No Clear Idea	25 (50.0)	25 (50.0)	50		
Unemployability	43 (52.4)	39 (47.6)	82		
Others	7 (59.1)	15 (40.9)	22		
Total	169	146	315		

@ Denotes not significant

Sub-hypothesis 5.8

There is no association between educational qualifications and educational-related factors as a reason for the dropouts.

As per Table 4.52 the P-value is greater than 0.05 levels; there is no association between the student's educational qualification and the educational-related factors as a reason for the dropouts from the distance education institution. Therefore, the null hypothesis is accepted.

Table 4.52

Chi-square Test for Association between Educational Qualifications and Educational Factors

Educational factors	*Educational qualifications*				
	U.G	*P.G*	*Total*	*Chi Square Value*	*P-Value*
Hard Syllabus	36 (59.0)	25 (41.0)	61		
Lack of Library	21 (77.8)	6 (22.2)	27		
Less Memory	30 (69.8)	13 (30.2)	43		
Less Information	16 (53.3)	14 (46.7)	30	6.231	0.397@
No Clear Idea	28 (56.0)	22 (44.0)	50		
Unemployability	48 (58.5)	34 (41.5)	82		
Others	14 (63.6)	8 (36.4)	22		
Total	193	122	315		

@ Denotes not significant

It is observed that irrespective of the student's educational qualifications (undergraduate / postgraduate level), all have a similar kind of educational-related factors as a reason for the dropouts.

Sub-hypothesis 5.9

There is no association between the university studied and the educational factor as a reason for the dropouts.

As per Table 4.53 the P-value is in association between the students who have studied in different universities and the educational-related factors as a reason for the dropouts from the distance education stream. Therefore, the null hypothesis is rejected.

Table 4.53

Chi-square Test for Association between Universities Studied and Educational Factors

Education factors	*University studied*			*Total*	*Chi Square Value*	*P-Value*
	Madras University	*Bharathi-dasan University*	*Madurai Kamaraj University*			
Hard Syllabus	20 (32.8)	19 (31.1)	22 (36.1)	61		
Lack of Library	17 (63.0)	6 (22.2)	4 (14.8)	27		
Less Memory	10 (23.2)	15 (34.9)	18 (41.9)	43		
Less Information	13 (43.3)	7 (23.3)	10 (33.3)	30	25.272	0.013*
No Clear Idea	24 (48.0)	15 (30.0)	11 (22.0)	50		
Unemployability	37 (45.1)	22 (26.8)	23 (28.0)	82		
Other	5 (22.7)	13 (59.1)	4 (18.2)	22		
Total	126	97	92	315		

* Significant at 0.05 per cent level

It is observed that students belonging to different universities had different kinds of educational-related factors as a reason for the dropouts.

Sub-hypothesis 5.10

There is no association between employment status of dropouts and the education-related factors as a reason for the dropouts.

As per Table 4.54 the P-value is significant between the employment status of dropouts and the educational-related factors as a reason for the dropouts from the distance education stream. Therefore, the null hypothesis is rejected.

It is observed that the employment status of the dropout plays a role in association with the educational-related factors as a reason for the dropouts.

Table 4.54

Chi-square Test for Association between Employment Status and Educational Factors

	Employment status				
Educational factors	*Employed*	*Unemployed*	*Total*	*Chi Square Value*	*P-Value Hard*
Syllabus	45 (73.8)	16 (26.2)	61		
Lack of Library	20 (74.1)	7 (25.9)	27		
Less Memory	23 (53.5)	20 (46.5)	43		
Less Information	25 (83.3)	5 (16.7)	30	15.834	0.014*
No Clear Idea	34 (68.0)	16 (32.0)	50		
Unemployability	53 (64.6)	29 (35.4)	82		
Others	9 (40.9)	13 (59.1)	22		
Total	209	106	315		

*Significant at 0.05 per cent level

Sub-hypothesis 5.11

There is no association between the annual income of the family of the dropouts and the education-related factors as a reason for the dropouts.

As per Table 4.55 the P-value is in association between the family's annual income and the educational-related factors at 0.01 per cent level as a reason for the dropouts from the distance education stream. Therefore, the null hypothesis is rejected.

It is observed that the dropouts' family's annual income plays a vital role in association with the educational-related factors as a reason for the dropouts.

Table 4.55

Chi-square Test for Association between Family's Annual Income and Educational Factors

	Family's annual income (in rupees)					
Educational factors	*Below 20,000*	*20,000-30,000*	*Above 30,000*	*Total*	*Chi Square Value*	*P-Value*
Hard Syllabus	12 (19.7)	31 (50.8)	18 (29.5)	61		
Lack of Library	4 (14.8)	8 (29.6)	15 (55.6)	27		
Less Memory	7 (16.3)	14 (32.6)	22 (51.2)	43		
Less Information	5 (16.7)	17 (56.7)	8 (26.7)	30	31.190	0.001**
No Clear Idea	14 (28.0)	6 (12.0)	30 (60.0)	50		
Unemployability	23 (28.0)	25 (30.5)	34 (41.5)	82		
Others	3 (13.6)	8 (36.4)	11 (50.0)	22		
Total	68	109	138	315		

** Significant at 0.01 per cent level

Major Hypothesis 6

There will be no association between employment factors and personal attributions.

Sub-hypothesis 6.1

There is no association between the age group and the employment factor as a reason for the dropouts.

Table 4.56

Chi-square Test for Association between Age Group and Employment-related Factors

Employment factors	*Age group* 18 - 22	23 - 27	Above 27	*Total*	*Chi Square Value*	*P - Value*
Heavy Work in Office	11 (13.1)	32 (38.1)	41 (48.8)	84		
Promotion	9 (14.8)	28 (45.9)	24 (39.3)	61		
Transfer to Other Places	3 (7.0)	29 (67.4)	11 (25.6)	43	23.208	0.003**
Change of Work	3 (10.0)	16 (53.3)	11 (36.7)	30		
Unemployment	25 (25.8)	48 (49.5)	24 (24.7)	97		
Total	51	153	111	315		

* * Significant at 0.01 per cent level

As per Table 4.56 the P-value is significant at 0.01 per cent levels; there is an association between the age group of the dropouts and their employment-related factors as a reason for the dropouts from the distance education institution.

Therefore, the null hypothesis is rejected. The analysis reveals that the influence of employment factors on different age groups is the reasons for the dropouts.

Sub-hypothesis 6.2

There is no association between sex and the employment factor as a reason for dropouts.

As per Table 4.57 the P-value is significant at 0.01 per cent levels; there is association between the sex and the employment-related factors as a reason for the dropouts from the distance education institution.

Therefore, the null hypothesis is rejected. It was observed that the sex of the dropouts plays a vital role in association with the employment-related factors as a reason for the dropouts.

Table 4.57: Chi-square Test for Association between Sex and Employment Related-factors

Employment factors	*Sex*				
	Male	*Female*	*Total*	*Chi Square Value*	*P-Value*
Heavy Work in Office	60 (71.4)	24 (28.6)	84		
Promotion	43 (70.5)	18 (29.5)	61		
Transfer to Other Places	31 (72.1)	12 (27.9)	43	25.534	0.000**
Change of Work	24 (80.0)	6 (20.0)	30		
Unemployment	42 (43.3)	55 (56.7)	97		
Total	200	115	315		

* * Significant at 0.01 per cent level

Sub-hypothesis 6.3

There is no association between the marital status and the employment-related factor as a reason for the dropouts.

Table 4.58: Chi-square Test for Association between Marital Status and Employment Related-factors

Employment factors	*Marital status*				
	Married	*Unmarried*	*Total*	*Chi Square Value*	*P-Value*
Heavy Work in Office	38 (45.2)	46 (54.8)	84		
Promotion	34 (55.7)	27 (44.3)	61		
Transfer to Other Places	23 (53.5)	20 (46.5)	43	3.278	0.512@
Change of Work	12 (40.0)	18 (60.0)	30		
Unemployment	44 (45.4)	53 (54.6)	97		
Total	151	164	315		

@ Denotes not significant

As per Table 4.58 the P-value is not significant; there is no association between the marital status of the dropouts and their employment-related factors as a reason for the dropouts from the distance education institution.

Therefore, the null hypothesis is accepted. It is observed that the marital status of the dropouts did not influence in association with the employment-related factors as a reason for the dropouts.

Sub-hypothesis 6.4

There is no association between the type of family and the employment-related factors as a reason for the dropouts.

Table 4.59

Chi-square Test for Association between the Type of Family and Employment-related Reactors

	Type of family				
Employment factors	*Nuclear*	*Joint*	*Total*	*Chi Square Value*	*P-Value*
Heavy work in office	24 (28.6)	60 (71.4)	84		
Promotion	22 (36.1)	39 (63.9)	61		
Transfer to other places	13 (30.2)	30 (69.8)	43		
Change of work	8 (26.7)	22 (73.3)	30	1.237	0.871@
Unemployment	30 (30.9)	67 (69.1)	97		
Total	97	218	315		

@ Denotes not significant

As per Table 4.59 the P-value is not significant; there is no association between the type of family and the employment-related factors as a reason for the dropouts from the distance education institution.

Therefore, the null hypothesis is accepted. It is observed that the type of family of the dropouts did not play any role in association with the employment-related factors as a reason for the dropouts.

Sub-hypothesis 6.5

There is no association between religion and the employment factor as a reason for the dropouts.

As per Table 4.60 the P-value is not significant; there is no association between the religion of the dropouts and the employment-related factors as a reason for the dropouts from the distance education institution.

Table 4.60

Chi-square Test for Association between Religion and Employment-related Factors

	Religion					
Employment factors	*Hindu*	*Muslim*	*Christian*	*Total*	*Chi Square Value*	*P-Value*
Heavy work in office	54 (64.3)	20 (23.8)	10 (11.9)	84		
Promotion	35 (57.4)	16 (26.2)	10 (16.4)	61		
Transfer to other places	25 (58.1)	11 (25.6)	7 (16.3)	43		
Change of work	17 (56.7)	7 (23.3)	6 (20.0)	30	3.686	0.884@
Unemployment	63 (64.9)	17 (17.5)	17 (17.5)	97		
Total	194	71	50	315		

@ Denotes not significant

Therefore, the null hypothesis is accepted. It is observed that religion of the dropouts does not play a major role as a reason for the dropout.

Sub-hypothesis 6.6

There is no association between community and the employment factor as a reason for the dropouts.

As per Table 4.61 the P-value is significant at 0.01 per cent levels; there is an association between the community of the dropouts and the employment related factors as a reason for dropouts from the distance education institution.

Therefore, the null hypothesis is rejected. It is observed that the community of the dropouts and their employment-related factors are the pertinent reasons for the dropouts.

Sub-hypothesis 6.7

There is no association between the place of birth and the employment-related factors as a reason for the dropouts.

Table 4.61

Chi-square Test for Association between Community and Employment-related Factors

	Community						
Employment factors	*B.C*	*M.B.C*	*SC/ST*	*OC*	*Total*	*Chi Square Value*	*P - Value*
Heavy Work in Office	37 (44.0)	30 (35.7)	11 (13.1)	6 (7.1)	84		
Promotion	33 (54.1)	7 (11.5)	9 (14.8)	12 (19.7)	61		
Transfer to Other Places	22 (51.2)	11 (25.6)	9 (20.9)	1 (2.3)	43		
Change of Work	10 (33.3)	8 (26.7)	8 (26.7)	4 (13.3)	30	27.815	0.005**
Unemployment	45 (46.4)	23 (23.7)	24 (24.7)	5 (5.2)	97		
Total	147	79	61	28	315		

* * Significant at 0.01 per cent level

As per Table 4.62 the P-value is not significant; there is no association between the place of birth of the dropout and the employment related factors as a reason for the dropouts from the distance education institution.

Table 4.62

Chi-square Test for Association between Place of Birth and Employment-related Factors

Employment factors	*Place of birth*				
	Urban	*Rural*	*Total*	*Chi Square Value*	*P-Value*
Heavy Work in Office	41 (48.8)	43 (51.2)	84		
Promotion	38 (62.3)	23 (37.7)	61		
Transfer to Other Places	18 (41.9)	25 (58.1)	43		
Change of Work	15 (50.0)	15 (50.0)	30	6.208	0.184@
Unemployment	57 (58.8)	40 (41.2)	97		
Total	169	146	315		

@ Denotes not significant

Therefore, the null hypothesis is accepted. It is observed that the place of birth of the dropouts did not play a vital role in association with the employment-related factors as a reason for the dropouts.

Sub-hypothesis 6.8

There is no association between the educational qualification and the employment factor as a reason for the dropouts.

As per Table 4.63 the P-value is not significant; there is no association between the educational qualifications and the employment-related factors as a reason for the dropouts from the distance education institution.

Therefore, the null hypothesis is accepted. It was observed that the educational qualification of the dropouts plays a vital role in association with the employment-related factors as a reason for the dropout.

Table 4.63: Chi-square Test for Association between Educational Qualification and Employment-related Factors

Employment factors	*Educational qualifications*				
	U.G	*P.G*	*Total*	*Chi Square Value*	*P-Value*
Heavy Work in Office	52 (61.9)	32 (38.1)	84		
Promotion	33 (54.1)	28 (45.9)	61		
Transfer to Other Places	26 (60.5)	17 (39.5)	43	1.935	0.744@
Change of Work	19 (63.3)	11 (36.7)	30		
Unemployment	63 (64.9)	34 (35.1)	97		
Total	193	122	315		

@ Denotes not significant

***Sub-hypothesis* 6.9**

There is no association between the university studied and the employment-related factor as a reason for the dropouts.

Table 4.64: Chi-square Test for Association between Universities Studied and Employment-related Factors

	University studied					
Employment factors	*Madras University*	*Bharathi-dasan University*	*Madurai Kamaraj University*	*Total*	*Chi Square Value*	*P-Value*
Heavy Work in Office	31 (36.9)	32 (38.1)	21 (25.0)	84		
Promotion	28 (45.9)	10 (16.4)	23 (37.7)	61		
Transfer to Other Places	22 (51.2)	6 (14.0)	15 (34.9)	43		
Change of Work	16 (53.3)	5 (16.7)	9 (30.0)	30	27.191	0.000**
Unemployment	29 (29.9)	44 (45.4)	24 (24.7)	97		
Total	126	97	92	315		

** Significant at 0.01 per cent level

As per Table 4.64 the P-value is significant at 0.01 per cent levels; there is association between the university studied and the employment-related factors as a reason for the dropouts from the distance education institution.

Therefore, the null hypothesis is rejected. It is observed that the university studied in association with the employment-related factors of the dropout plays a vital role as a reason for the dropouts.

Sub-hypothesis 6.10

There is no association between employment status and the employment-related factors as a reason for the dropouts.

Table 4.65

Chi-square Test for Association between Employment Status and Employment-related Factors

	Employment status				
Employment factors	*Employed*	*Unemployed*	*Total*	*Chi Square Value*	*P-Value*
Heavy Work in Office	84 (100.0)	0 (00.0)	84		
Promotion	48 (78.7)	13 (21.3)	61		
Transfer to Other Places	35 (81.4)	8 (18.6)	43		
Change of Work	24 (80.0)	6 (20.0)	30	152.86	0.000**
Unemployment	18 (18.6)	79 (81.4)	97		
Total	209	106	315		

* * Significant at 0.01 per cent level

As per Table 4.65 the P-value is significant at 0.01 per cent levels; there is an association between the employment status and the employment-related factors as a reason for the dropouts from the distance education institution.

Therefore, the null hypothesis is rejected. It is observed that the employment status of the dropouts and the employment-related factors play a vital role as a reason for the dropouts.

Sub-hypothesis 6.11

There is no association between a family's annual income and the employment-related factors as a reason for the dropouts.

Table 4.66: Chi-square Test for Association between Family's Annual Income and Employment-related Factors

	Family's annual income (in rupees)					
Educational factors	*Below 20,000*	*20,000-30,000*	*Above 30,000*	*Total*	*Chi Square Value*	*P-Value*
Heavy Work in Office	12 (14.3)	35 (41.7)	37 (44.0)	84		
Promotion	15 (24.6)	22 (36.1)	24 (39.3)	61		
Transfer to Other Places	10 (23.3)	19 (44.2)	14 (32.6)	43	21.882	0.005**
Change of Work	13 (43.3)	9 (30.0)	8 (26.7)	30		
Unemployment	18 (18.6)	24 (24.7)	55 (56.7)	97		
Total	68	109	138	315		

* * Significant at 0.01 per cent level

As per Table 4.66 the P-value is significant at 0.01 per cent levels; there is an association between the family's annual income and the employment-related factors as a reason for the dropouts from the distance education institution.

Therefore, the null hypothesis is rejected. It is observed that the family's annual income of the dropout plays an important role for the dropouts in distance education stream.

Major Hypothesis 7

There will be no association between economic-related factors and personal attributions.

Sub-hypothesis 7.1

There is no association between age group and economic factors as a reason for the dropouts.

Table 4.67

Chi-square Test for Association between Age Group and Economic-related Factors

Economic factors	*Age group* 18 - 22	23 - 27	Above 27	Total	*Chi Square Value*	*P - Value*
Tuition Fees is high	12 (20.0)	21 (35.0)	27 (45.0)	60		
Unable to Bear the Tuition Fees	13 (15.3)	40 (47.1)	32 (37.6)	85		
Unable to bear the Exam Fees	8 (14.3)	27 (42.2)	21 (37.5)	56	11.29	0.185@
Non-availability of Scholarship	14 (17.5)	48 (60.0)	18 (22.5)	80		
Others	4 (11.8)	17 (50.0)	13 (38.2)	34		
Total	51	153	111	315		

@ Denotes not significant

As per Table 4.67 the P-value is not significant; there is no association between the age group and the economic-related factors as a reason for the dropouts from the distance education institution.

Therefore, the null hypothesis is accepted. It was observed that the age group of the dropouts does not play a vital role in association with the economic-related factors as a reason for the dropouts.

Sub-hypothesis 7.2

There is no association between sex and economic-related factors as a reason for the dropouts.

Table 4.68: Chi-square Test for Association between Sex and Economic-related Factors

	Sex				
Economic factors	*Male*	*Female*	*Total*	*Chi Square Value*	*P-Value*
Tuition Fees is High	37 (61.7)	23 (38.3)	60		
Unable to Bear the Tuition Fees	55 (64.7)	30 (35.3)	85		
Unable to Bear the Exam Fees	37 (66.1)	19 (33.9)	56		
Non-availability of Scholarship	50 (62.5)	30 (37.5)	80	0.378	0.984@
Others	21 (61.8)	13 (38.2)	34		
Total	200	115	315		

@ Denotes not significant

Table 4.69: Chi-square Test for Association between Marital Status and Economic-related Factors

	Marital status				
Economic factors	*Married*	*Unmarried*	*Total*	*Chi Square Value*	*P-Value*
Tuition Fees is High	32 (53.3)	28 (46.7)	60		
Unable to Bear the Tuition Fees	47 (55.3)	38 (44.7)	85		
Unable to Bear the Exam Fees	25 (44.6)	31 (55.4)	56		
Non-availability of Scholarship	24 (30.0)	56 (70.0)	80	18.392	0.001**
Others	23 (67.6)	11 (32.4)	34		
Total	151	164	315		

* * Significant at 0.01 per cent level

As per Table 4.68 the P-value is not significant; there is no association between sex and economic-related factors as a reason for the dropouts from the distance education institution.

Therefore, the null hypothesis is accepted. It is observed that the gender of the dropouts does not play a vital role in association with the economic-related factors as a reason for the dropouts.

Sub-hypothesis 7.3

There is no association between marital status and the economic-related factors as a reason for the dropouts.

Table 4.70

Chi-square Test for Association between the Type of Family and Economic-related Factors

	Type of family				
Economic factors	*Nuclear*	*Joint*	*Total*	*Chi Square Value*	*P-Value*
Tuition Fees is High	18 (30.0)	40.2 (70.0)	60		
Unable to Bear the Tuition Fees	26 (30.6)	59 (69.4)	85		
Unable to Bear the Exam Fees	23 (41.1)	33 (58.9)	56	4.696	0.319@
Non-availability of Scholarship	19 (23.8)	61 (76.3)	80		
Others	11 (32.4)	23 (67.6)	34		
Total	97	218	315		

@ Denotes not significant

As per Table 4.69 the P-value is significant at 0.01 per cent level; there is an association between the marital status of the dropouts and the economic-related factors as a reason for the dropouts from the distance education institution.

Therefore, the null hypothesis is rejected. It is observed that the marital status of the dropouts plays a vital role in association with the economic-related factors as a reason for the dropouts.

Sub-hypothesis 7.4

There is no association between the type of family and the economic-related factors as a reason for the dropouts.

As per Table 4.70 the P-value is greater than 0.05 levels; there is no association between the type of family and the economic-related factors as a reason for the dropouts from the distance education institution.

Table 4.71: Chi-square Test for Association between Religion and Economic-related Factors

Economic factors	*Religion*					
	Hindu	*Muslim*	*Christian*	*Total*	*Chi Square Value*	*P-Value*
Tuition Fees is High	31 (51.7)	19 (31.7)	10 (16.7)	60		
Unable to Bear the Tuition Fees	50 (58.8)	20 (23.5)	15 (17.6)	85		
Unable to Bear the Exam Fees	31 (55.4)	15 (26.8)	10 (17.9)	56	10.65	0.221@
Non-availability of Scholarship	57 (71.3)	11 (13.8)	12 (15.0)	80		
Others	25 (73.5)	6 (17.6)	3 (8.8)	34		
Total	194	71	50	315		

@ Denotes not significant

Therefore, the null hypothesis is accepted. It is observed that the type of family of the dropouts did not play a vital role in association with the economic-related factors as a reason for the dropouts.

Sub-hypothesis 7.5

There is no association between religion and economic-related factors as a reason for the dropouts.

As per Table 4.71 the P-value is not significant; there is no association between the religion of the dropouts and the economic-related factors as a reason for the dropouts from the distance education institution.

Therefore, the null hypothesis is accepted. It is observed that religion and economic-related factors do not play a major role in dropping out from the distance education stream.

Sub-hypothesis 7.6

There is no association between communities and the economic-related factors as a reason for the dropouts.

Table 4.72

Chi-square Test for Association between Communities and Economic-related factors

Economic factors	*Community*						
	B.C	*M.B.C*	*SC/ST*	*OC*	*Total*	*Chi Square Value*	*P - Value*
Tuition Fees is High	29 (48.3)	17 (28.3)	14 (23.3)	0	60		
Unable to Bear the Tuition Fees	40 (47.1)	18 (21.2)	16 (18.8)	11 (12.9)	85		
Unable to bear the Exam Fees	28 (50.0)	9 (16.1)	11 (19.6)	8 (14.3)	56		
Non-availability of Scholarship	32 (40.0)	29 (36.3)	11 (13.8)	8 (10.0)	80	21.426	0.044@
Others	18 (52.9)	6 (17.6)	9 (26.5)	1 (2.9)	34		
Total	147	79	61	28	315		

@ Denotes not significant

As per Table 4.72 the P-value is not significant; there is no association between the community of the dropouts and the economic-related factors as a reason for dropouts from the distance education institution.

Therefore, the null hypothesis is accepted. It is observed that the community of the dropouts did not play a vital role in association with the economic-related factors as a reason for the dropouts.

Sub-hypothesis 7.7

There is no association between the place of birth and the economic-related factors as a reason for the dropouts.

Table 4.73

Chi-square Test for Association between Places of Birth and Economic-related factors

	Place of birth				
Economic factors	*Urban*	*Rural*	*Total*	*Chi Square Value*	*P-Value*
Tuition Fees is High	34 (56.7)	26 (43.3)	60		
Unable to Bear the Tuition Fees	39 (45.9)	46 (54.1)	85		
Unable to Bear the Exam Fees	33 (58.9)	23 (41.1)	56		
Non-availability of Scholarship	48 (60.0)	32 (40.0)	80	5.449	0.244@
Others	15 (44.1)	19 (55.9)	34		
Total	169	146	315		

@ Denotes not significant

As per Table 4.73 the P-value is greater than 0.05 levels; there is no association between the place of birth of dropouts and the economic-related factors as a reason for the dropouts from the distance education institution.

Therefore, the null hypothesis is accepted. It is observed that the place of birth of the dropouts did not play a vital role in association with the economic-related factors as a reason for the dropouts.

Sub-hypothesis 7.8

There is no association between the educational qualifications and the economic factors as a reason for the dropouts.

Table 4.74

Chi-square Test for

Association between Educational Qualifications and Economic-related Factors

Economic factors	*Educational qualifications*				
	U.G	*P.G*	*Total*	*Chi Square Value*	*P-Value*
Tuition Fees is High	51 (85.0)	9 (15.0)	60		
Unable to Bear the Tuition Fees	55 (64.7)	30 (35.3)	85		
Unable to Bear the Exam Fees	32 (57.1)	24 (42.9)	56		
Non-availability of Scholarship	37 (46.3)	43 (53.8)	80	23.662	0.000**
Others	18 (52.9)	16 (47.1)	34		
Total	193	122	315		

* * Significant at 0.01 per cent level

As per Table 4.74 the P-value is significant at 0.01 per cent level; there is an association between the educational qualification of the dropouts and their economic-related factors as a reason for dropouts from the distance education institution.

Therefore, the null hypothesis is rejected. It is observed that the educational qualification and economic factors of the students play a vital role in dropping out from the distance education stream.

Sub-hypothesis 7.9

There is no association between the university studied and the economic factors as a reason for the dropouts.

Table 4.75

Chi-square Test for Association between Universities Studied and Economic-related Factors

	University studied					
Economic Factors	*Madras University*	*Bharathi-dasan University*	*Madurai Kamaraj University*	*Total*	*Chi Square Value*	*P-Value*
Tuition Fees is High	29 (48.3)	14 (23.3)	17 (28.3)	60		
Unable to Bear the Tuition Fees	41 (48.2)	21 (24.7)	23 (27.1)	85		
Unable to Bear the Exam Fees	21 (37.5)	9 (16.1)	26 (46.4)	56		
Non-availability of Scholarship	18 (22.5)	45 (56.3)	17 (21.3)	80	40.670	0.000**
Others	17 (50.0)	8 (23.5)	9 (26.5)	34		
Total	126	97	92	315		

* * Significant at 0.01 per cent level

As per Table 4.75 the P-value is significant at 0.01 per cent level; there is association between the university in which the dropouts studied and the economic-related factors as a reason for dropouts from the distance education institution.

Therefore, the null hypothesis is rejected. The analysis concluded that there is a close association between economic factors and the student dropouts in the distance education stream. Economic factors are the axial factors as a reason for the dropouts.

Sub-hypothesis 7.10

There is no association between the employment status and the economic-related factors as a reason for the dropouts.

As per Table 4.76 the P-value is not significant; there is no association between the employment status of the dropouts and the economic-related factors as a reason for the dropouts from the distance education institution.

Therefore, the null hypothesis is accepted. It was observed that the employment status of the dropouts did not play a vital role in association with the economic-related factors as a reason for the dropouts.

Table 4.76

Chi-square Test for Association between Employment Status and Economic-related Factors

	Employment status				
Economic factors	*Employed*	*Unemployed*	*Total*	*Chi Square Value*	*P-Value*
Tuition Fees is High	39 (65.0)	21 (35.0)	60		
Unable to Bear the Tuition Fees	56 (65.9)	29 (34.1)	85		
Unable to Bear the Exam Fees	39 (69.6)	17 (30.4)	56		
Non-availability of Scholarship	52 (65.0)	28 (35.0)	80	0.420	0.980@
Others	23 (67.6)	11 (32.4)	34		
Total	209	106	315		

@ Denotes not significant

Sub-hypothesis 7.11

There is no association between the annual income of the family and the economic-related factors as a reason for the dropouts.

As per Table 4.77 the P-value is significant at 0.01 per cent level; there is an association between the family's annual income of the dropouts and the economic-related factors as a reason for the dropouts from the distance education institution.

Therefore, the null hypothesis is rejected. It is observed that the family's annual income plays a vital role in association with the economic-related factors as a reason for the dropouts.

Major Hypothesis 8

There will be no association between institutional-related factors and personal attributions.

Sub-hypothesis 8.1

There is no association between the age group and the institutional factors as a reason for the dropouts.

Table 4.77

Chi-square Test for Association between Family's Annual Income and Economic-related Factors

	Family's annual income (in rupees)					
Economic factors	*Below 20,000*	*20,000-30,000*	*Above 30,000*	*Total*	*Chi Square Value*	*P-Value*
Tuition Fees is High	20 (33.3)	14 (23.3)	26 (43.3)	60		
Unable to Bear the Tuition Fees	19 (22.4)	23 (27.1)	43 (50.6)	85		
Unable to Bear the Exam Fees	6 (10.7)	26 (46.4)	24 (42.9)	56	26.987	0.000**
Non-availability of Scholarship	15 (18.8)	40 (50.0)	25 (31.3)	80		
Others	8 (23.5)	6 (17.6)	20 (58.8)	34		
Total	68	109	138	315		

* * Significant at 0.01 per cent level

As per Table 4.78 the P-value is significant at 0.05 levels. There is an association between the age group of the dropouts and institutional-related factors as a reason for the dropouts from the distance education institution. Therefore, the null hypothesis is rejected. It is observed that the age group of the dropouts plays a vital role in association with the institutional-related factors as a reason for the dropouts.

Table 4.78

Chi-square Test for Association between Age Group and Institutional Factors

Institutional factors	*Age group* 18 - 22	23 - 27	Above 27	*Total*	*Chi Square Value*	*P - Value*
Delay in receipt of study materials	3 (9.1)	16 (48.5)	14 (42.4)	33		
Failure to dispatch study materials	7 (28.0)	7 (28.0)	11 (44.0)	25		
Long distance to study centre/PCP	4 (8.9)	30 (66.7)	11 (24.4)	45		
Lack of information at PCP	4 (12.5)	20 (62.5)	8 (25.0)	32		
High tuition fees	14 (21.2)	27 (40.9)	25 (37.9)	66		
Lack of public relation	4 (22.2)	9 (50.0)	5 (27.8)	18	28.845	0.025*
No answer to postal queries	1 (3.1)	15 (46.9)	16 (50.0)	32		
Unsatisfactory reply to personal queries	9 (19.1)	25 (53.2)	13 (27.7)	47		
Others	5 (29.4)	4 (23.5)	8 (47.1)	17		
Total	51	153	111	315		

* Significant at 0.05 per cent level

Sub-hypothesis 8.2

There is no association between sex and institutional factors as a reason for the dropouts.

Table 4.79

Chi-square Test for Association between Sex and Institutional Factors

Institutional factors	*Sex*				
	Male	*Female*	*Total*	*Chi Square Value*	*P-Value*
Delay in receipt of study materials	19 (57.6)	14 (42.4)	33		
Failure to dispatch study materials	16 (64.0)	9 (36.0)	25		
Long distance to study centre/PCP	29 (64.4)	16 (35.6)	45		
Lack of information at PCP	18 (56.3)	14 (43.8)	32		
High tuition fees	45 (68.2)	21 (31.8)	66		
Lack of public relation	12 (66.7)	6 (33.3)	18	3.986	0.858@
No answer to postal queries	21 (65.6)	11 (34.4)	32		
Unsatisfactory reply to personal queries	27 (57.4)	20 (42.6)	47		
Others	13 (76.5)	4 (23.5)	17		
Total	200	115	315		

@ Denotes not significant

As per Table 4.79 the P-value is greater than 0.05 levels; there is no association between sex and institutional-related factors as a reason for the dropouts from the distance education institution. Therefore, the null hypothesis is accepted. It is observed that the sex of the dropout did not play a vital role in association with the institutional related factors as a reason for dropouts.

Sub-hypothesis 8.3

There is no association between the marital status and the institutional factors as a reason for the dropouts.

Table 4.80

Chi-square Test for Association between Marital Status and Institutional Factors

Institutional factors	*Marital Status*				
	Married	*Unmarried*	*Total*	*Chi Square Value*	*P-Value*
Delay in receipt of study materials	15 (45.5)	18 (54.6)	33		
Failure to dispatch study materials	12 (48.00)	13 (52.00)	25		
Long distance to study centre/PCP	21 (46.7)	24 (53.33)	45		
Lack of information at PCP	13 (40.63)	19 (59.4)	32		
High tuition fees	32 (48.5)	34 (51.52)	66		
Lack of public relation	4 (22.22)	14 (77.8)	18	9.324	0.315@
No answer to postal queries	20 (62.50)	12 (37.50)	32		
Unsatisfactory reply to personal queries	26 (55.32)	21 (44.7)	47		
Others	8 (47.06)	9 (52.94)	17		
Total	151	164	315		

@ Denotes not significant

As per Table 4.80 the P-value is greater than 0.05 levels; there is no association between the marital status and the institutional-related factors as a reason for the dropouts from the distance education institution. Therefore, the null hypothesis is accepted. It is observed that marital status of the dropouts did not play a vital role in association with the institutional-related factors as a reason for the dropouts.

Sub-hypothesis 8.4

There is no association between the type of family and the institutional factors as a reason for the dropouts.

Table 4.81

Chi-square Test for Association between the Type of Family and Institutional Factors

	Type of family				
Institutional factors	*Nuclear*	*Joint*	*Total*	*Chi Square Value*	*P-Value*
Delay in receipt of study materials	4 (12.12)	29 (87.9)	33		
Failure to dispatch study materials	11 (44.00)	14 (56.00)	25		
Long distance to study centre/PCP	13 (28.9)	32 (71.11)	45		
Lack of information at PCP	10 (31.25)	22 (68.75)	32		
High tuition fees	22 (33.33)	44 (66.7)	66	14.559	0.068@
Lack of public relation	5 (27.8)	13 (72.22)	18		
No answer to postal queries	16 (50.00)	16 (50.00)	32		
Unsatisfactory reply to personal queries	11 (23.40)	36 (76.60)	47		
Other	5 (100)	12 (70.6)	17		
Total	97	218	315		

@ Denotes not significant

As per Table 4.81 the P-value is significant at 0.05 levels; there is no association between the type of family and the institutional-related factors as a reason for the dropouts from the distance education institution. Therefore, the null hypothesis is accepted. It was observed that the type of family of the dropouts did not play a vital role in association with the institutional related factors as a reason for the dropouts.

Sub-hypothesis 8.5

There is no association between religion and institutional factors as a reason for the dropouts.

Table 4.82

Chi-square Test for Association between Religion and Institutional Factors

	Religion					
Institutional factors	*Hindu*	*Muslim*	*Christian*	*Total*	*Chi Square Value*	*P-Value*
Delay in receipt of study materials	20 (60.6)	5 (15.2)	8 (24.2)	33		
Failure to dispatch study materials	13 (52.0)	4 (16.0)	8 (32.0)	25		
Long distance to study centre/PCP	33 (73.3)	10 (22.2)	2 (4.4)	45		
Lack of information at PCP	22 (68.8)	6 (18.8)	4 (12.5)	32		
High tuition fees	33 (50.0)	20 (30.3)	13 (19.7)	66	27.065	0.040*
Lack of public relation	7 (38.9)	6 (33.3)	5 (27.8)	18		
No answer to postal queries	19 (59.4)	10 (31.3)	3 (9.4)	32		
Unsatisfactory reply to personal queries	35 (74.5)	8 (17.0)	4 (8.5)	47		
Others	12 (70.6)	2 (11.8)	3 (17.6)	17		
Total	194	71	50	315		

* Significant at 0.05 per cent level

As per Table 4.82 the P-value is greater than 0.05 levels; there is an association between religion and institutional-related factors as a reason for the dropouts from the distance education institution. Therefore, the null hypothesis is rejected. It is observed that the religion of the dropouts plays a vital role in association with the institutional-related factors as a reason for the dropouts.

Table 4.83

Chi-square Test for Association between Community and Institutional Factors

Institutional factors	*Community* B.C	M.B.C	SC/ST	OC	*Total*	*Chi Square Value*	*P - Value*
Delay in receipt of study materials	15 (45.5)	8 (24.2)	8 (24.2)	2 (6.1)	33		
Failure to dispatch study materials	12 (48.0)	7 (28.0)	4 (16.0)	2 (8.0)	25		
Long distance to study centre/PCP	20 (44.4)	15 (33.3)	7 (15.6)	3 (6.7)	45		
Lack of information at PCP	15 (46.9)	5 (15.6)	9 (28.1)	3 (9.4)	32		
High tuition fees	32 (48.5)	9 (13.6)	18 (27.3)	7 (10.6)	66		
Lack of public relation	5 (27.8)	11 (61.1)	2 (11.1)	0 (00.0)	18	45.928	0.004**
No answer to postal queries	15 (46.9)	4 (12.5)	6 (18.8)	7 (21.9)	32		
Unsatisfactory reply to personal queries	27 (57.4)	10 (21.3)	6 (12.8)	4 (8.5)	47		
Others	6 (35.3)	10 (58.8)	1 (5.9)	0 (00.0)	17		
Total	147	79	61	28	315		

** Significant at 0.01 per cent level

Table 4.84

Chi-square Test for Association between Place of Birth and Institutional Factors

Institutional factors	*Place of birth* Urban	Rural	Total	*Chi Square Value*	*P-Value*
Delay in receipt of study materials	20 (60.61)	13 (39.4)	33		
Failure to dispatch study materials	13 (52.00)	12 (48.00)	25		
Long distance to study centre/PCP	13 (28.9)	32 (71.11)	45		
Lack of information at PCP	18 (56.25)	14 (43.75)	32	16.617	0.034*
High tuition fees	40 (60.61)	26 (39.4)	66		
Lack of public relation	9 (50.00)	9 (50.00)	18		
No answer to postal queries	15 (46.9)	17 (53.13)	32		
Unsatisfactory reply to personal queries	30 (63.83)	17 (36.17)	47		
Others	11 (64.71)	6 (35.3)	17		
Total	169	146	315		

* Significant at 0.05 per cent level

Sub-hypothesis 8.6

There is no association between community and institutional factors as a reason for the dropouts.

As per Table 4.83 the P-value is significant at 0.01 levels; there is an association between the community and the institutional-related factors as a reason for the dropouts from the distance education institution. Therefore, the null hypothesis is rejected. It is observed that the community of the dropouts plays a vital role in association with the institutional-related factors as a reason for dropouts.

Table 4.85

Chi-square Test for Association between Educational Qualifications and Institutional Factors

Institutional factors	*Educational qualifications*				
	U.G	*P.G*	*Total*	*Chi Square Value*	*P-Value*
Delay in receipt of study materials	17 (51.5)	16 (48.5)	33		
Failure to dispatch study materials	21 (84.0)	4 (16.0)	25		
Long distance to study centre/PCP	32 (71.1)	13 (28.9)	45		
Lack of information at PCP	17 (53.1)	15 (46.9)	32		
High tuition fees	52 (78.8)	14 (21.1)	66	32.347	0.000**
Lack of public relation	9 (50.0)	9 (50.0)	18		
No answer to postal queries	10 (31.3)	22 (68)	32		
Unsatisfactory reply to personal queries	26 (55.3)	21 (44.7)	47		
Others	9 (52.9)	8 (47.1)	17		
Total	193	122	315		

* * Significant at 0.01 percent level

Sub-hypothesis 8.7

There is no association between the place of birth and the institutional factors as a reason for the dropouts.

As per Table 4.84 the P-value is significant at 0.05 levels; there is association between the place of birth and the institutional related factors as a reason for the dropouts from the distance education institution. Therefore, the null hypothesis is rejected.

Table 4.86

Chi-square Test for Association between Universities Studied and Institutional Factors

Institutional factors	*University studied*					
	Madras University	*Bharathidasan University*	*Madurai Kamaraj University*	*Total*	*Chi Square Value*	*P-Value*
Delay in receipt of study materials	16 (48.5)	11 (33.3)	6 (18.2)	33		
Failure to dispatch study materials	12 (48.0)	5 (20.0)	8 (32.0)	25		
Long distance to study centre/PCP	19 (42.2)	13 (28.9)	13 (28.9)	45		
Lack of information at PCP	10 (31.3)	11 (34.4)	11 (34.4)	32		
High tuition fees	27 (40.3)	21 (31.8)	18 (27.3)	66	24.312	0.082@
Lack of public relation	10 (55.6)	4 (22.2)	4 (22.2)	18		
No answer to postal queries	12 (37.5)	6 (18.8)	14 (43.8)	32		
Unsatisfactory reply to personal queries	19 (40.4)	14 (29.8)	14 (29.8)	47		
Others	1 (5.9)	12 (70.6)	4 (23.5)	17		
Total	126	97	92	315		

@ Denotes not significant

It is observed that the place of birth of the dropouts plays a vital role in association with the institutional-related factors as a reason for the dropouts.

Sub-hypothesis 8.8

There is no association between educational qualifications and institutional factors as a reason for the dropouts.

As per Table 4.85 the P-value is significant at 0.01 per cent level. There is an association between the educational qualification of the dropouts and the institutional-related factors as a reason for dropouts from the distance education institution. Therefore, the null hypothesis is rejected. It is observed that the educational qualification of the dropouts plays a vital role in association with the institutional-related factors as a reason for the dropouts.

Sub-hypothesis 8.9

There is no association between the university studied and the institutional factor as a reason for the dropouts.

As per Table 4.86 the P-value is greater than 0.05 levels; there is no association between the university studied and the institutional-related factors as a reason for the dropouts from the distance education institution. Therefore, the null hypothesis is accepted. It is observed that the student dropouts in distance education are not influenced by institutional-related factors as a reason for the dropouts. Different universities have different institutional factors as contributing factors for the dropouts.

Sub-hypothesis 8.10

There is no association between the employment status and the institutional factors as a reason for the dropouts.

As per Table 4.87 the P-value is greater than 0.05 levels; there is no association between the employment status and the institutional-related factors as a reason for the dropouts from the distance education institution. Therefore, the null hypothesis is accepted. It is observed that the employment status of the dropouts plays a vital role in association with the institutional-related factors as a reason for the dropouts.

Sub-hypothesis 8.11

There is no association between a family's annual income and the institutional factors as a reason for the dropouts.

Table 4.87

Chi-square Test for Association between Employment Status and Institutional Factor

Institutional factors	*Employment status*				
	Employed	*Unemployed*	*Total*	*Chi Square Value*	*P-Value*
Delay in receipt of study materials	21 (63.6)	12 (36.4)	33		
Failure to dispatch study materials	16 (64.0)	9 (36.0)	25		
Long distance to study centre/PCP	34 (75.6)	11 (24.4)	45		
Lack of information at PCP	26 (81.3)	6 (18.8)	32		
High tuition fees	47 (71.2)	19 (28.8)	66	13.596	0.092 @
Lack of public relation	10 (55.6)	8 (44.4)	18		
No answer to postal queries	22 (68.8)	10 (31.3)	32		
Unsatisfactory reply to personal queries	23 (48.9)	24 (51.1)	47		
Others	10 (58.8)	7 (41.2)	17		
Total	209	106	315		

@ Denotes not significant

As per Table 4.88 the P-value is significant at 0.01 levels; there is an association between the family's annual income and the institutional-related factors as a reason for the dropouts from the distance education institution. Therefore, the null hypothesis is rejected. It is observed that the family's annual income of the dropouts plays a vital role in association with the institutional-related factors as a reason for the dropouts.

□□□□□ 4.88

□□□□□□□□□□ □□□□ □□□ □□□□□□□□□□□ □□□□□□□ □□□□□□□□ □□□□□□ □□□□□□
□□□ □□□□□□□□□□□□□ □□□□□□□

□□□□□□□□ □□□□□□	□□□□□□□□ □□□□□□ □□□□□□ (□□ □□□□□□)					
	□□□□□ 20,000	20,000□ 30,000	□□□□□ 30,000	□□□□	□□□ □□□□□□ □□□□□	□□□□□□□
□□□□□ □□ □□□□□□□	5	9	19	33		
□□ □□□□□ □□□□□□□□□	(15.2)	(27.3)	(57.6)			
□□□□□□□ □□ □□□□□□□□	5	8	12	25		
□□□□□ □□□□□□□□□	(20.0)	(32.0)	(48.0)			
□□□□ □□□□□□□□ □□	9	16	20			
□□□□□ □□□□□□/□□□	(20.0)	(35.6)	(44.4)	45		
□□□□ □□ □□□□□□□□□□□	14	14	4	32		
□□ □□□	(43.8)	(43.8)	(12.5)			
□□□□ □□□□□□□ □□□□	17	11	38	66		
	(25.8)	(16.7)	(57.6)			
□□□□ □□ □□□□□□	2	11	5	18	49.828	0.000**
□□□□□□□□	(11.1)	(61.1)	(27.8)			
□□ □□□□□□ □□	10	14	8	32		
□□□□□□ □□□□□□□	(31.3)	(43.8)	(25.0)			
□□□□□□□□□□□□□□	5	15	27	47		
□□□□□ □□ □□□□□□□□	(10.6)	(31.9)	(57.4)			
□□□□□□□						
□□□□□□	1	11	5	17		
	(05.9)	(64.7)	(29.4)			
□□□□□	68	109	138	315		

** □□□□□□□□□□□ □□ 0.01 □□□ □□□□ □□□□□

Descriptive Analysis of Samples

After collection of the data, they was analysed by descriptive analysis to find out the reasons for the dropouts with regard to the socio-economic background of the learners.

Table 4.89

Frequency Distribution of Sample with Regard to Reasons for Dropouts

Reasons for dropouts	*Frequency in number*	*Percentage*
Psychological factors	28	8.89
Family factors	99	31.43
Social factors	05	01.59
Health factors	12	03.81
Educational factors	18	05.75
Employment factors	28	08.89
Economic Factors	83	26.35
Institutional Factors	42	13.33
Total	315	100.00

From Table 4.89, it is clearly visible that family factors (31.43 per cent) and economic factors (26.35 per cent) play the main role for the dropouts from the distance education stream; 13.33 per cent of the learners dropped outs due to institutional-related factors. Psychological-related factors (8.89 per cent) and their occupational related factors (8.89 per cent) also influenced the dropout. Compared to educational-related factors (5.75 per cent), the health-related factors (3.81 per cent) and social-related factors (1.59 per cent) influenced on a low level. Therefore, the family-related factors and economic-related factors are the main reasons for the dropouts from the distance education institutions.

Table : 4.90

Frequency Distribution of Sample with Regard to Willingness to Continue

Willingness to continue	*Frequency in number*	*Percentage*
Yes	200	63.49
No	115	36.51
Total	315	100.00

The Table 4.90 indicates that frequency distribution of the samples with regard to "willingness to continue their study", 63.49 per cent of the dropouts were willing to continue their study; 36.51 per cent of the dropouts were not willing to continue their study due to family and economic problems.

Therefore, if the distance education institutions arrange for the scholarship or educational loan for the dropouts they may show interest in continuing their studies.

5

Findings and Conclusion

This chapter deals with the consolidation of the findings presented in the previous chapter. The nature of the samples, major findings and conclusion are presented here.

Nature of the Samples

A majority of the samples (40 per cent) are taken from the dropouts belonging to Madras University. The samples from Bharathidasan University and Madurai Kamaraj University share more or less an equal percentage of the sample population, i.e., 30.79 per cent and 29.21 per cent.

As many as 60.27 per cent of the dropout students are at undergraduate level and 38.73 per cent at postgraduate level, 63.49 per cent of the sample constitutes male dropouts and 36.51 per cent sample female dropouts; 48.57 per cent of the samples fall in the age group of 23-27 and 35.24 per cent of the dropouts fall in the age group of above 27, and 16.19 per cent of the dropouts is in the age group of 18-23, 52.6 per cent of the samples are unmarried and 47.94 per cent of the samples are married.

According to the religion-wise distribution of samples, 61.59 per cent of the samples is from the Hindu religion, 22.54 per cent of the dropouts is from the Muslim religion and 15.87 per cent of the dropouts is from the Christian religion. According to the sample study, 46.67 per cent of the samples belong to the backward community, 25.08 per cent belong to the most backward community and 19.37 per cent of the samples belong to the SC/ST community and the least of the samples, 8.89 per cent belong to other communities.

It is found that 53.65 per cent of the samples of dropouts are from urban areas and 46.35 per cent are from rural areas; 69.21

per cent of the samples of dropouts are from the joint family system and 30.79 per cent are from the nuclear family. The respondents' fathers' education were studied and it was observed that 39.68 per cent of the father's educational qualification of the sample was between 9 and 12 standard, 9.84 per cent were graduates and professional-course-completed fathers. Illiterate fathers constituted 19.68 per cent; 30.79 per cent of the fathers had studied between first standard and eighth standard.

It was observed from the samples that most of the fathers had studied only up to the school level. Most of the mothers were illiterate and had studied up to middle school level. Only 4.13 per cent of mothers possessed graduate degrees; 17.78 per cent had studied up to higher secondary level; 35.56 per cent of the fathers' occupation was agricultural labourers and coolies and 26.03 per cent of fathers' occupation was in the government sector; 25.40 per cent of the fathers' occupation was business; 13.02 per cent of the fathers worked in the private sector; 35.24 per cent of the mothers were home makers; 29.84 per cent of the mothers work for daily wages. Employed and agricultural workers were more or less of the same percentages.

Employed dropouts were 66.35 per cent and unemployed dropout students were 33.65 per cent; 29.52 per cent of the learners worked in the private sector. 11.75 per cent of the dropouts work in government concerns. It is understood that most of the dropouts were employed people; 43.81 per cent of the samples' annual income of the family was above Rs. 30,000; 34.60 per cent of the samples' annual income of the family was Rs. 20,000 to Rs. 30, 000 and 21.59 per cent of the samples' annual income of the family was below Rs. 20,000.

Findings of Inferential Analyses on Sample

1. The following psychological factors are influencing as reasons for dropouts:

The analysis enlightens that students belonging to different universities had a similar kind of psychological factors, namely, no intention study further, less retention/memory power, fear of failure, inferiority complex and teasing by others as a reason for the dropouts. Sex of the sample and academic background of the students were influenced by the psychological factors as a reason for the dropouts. Students whose age group lies between was 18-22, 23-27 and above 27 were having different psychological factors as a reason for the dropouts. The analysis reveals that the age group 23-27 was more influenced by the psychological factors as a reason for the dropout than the age group of above 27. The annual income of the family played a major role as a reason for the dropouts. Annual income was a confronting factor for dropouts.

2. The following psychological factors were not reasons for dropouts:

There was no relationship between psychological factors and personal attributes. The students' community, namely, backward, most backward, scheduled cast or scheduled tribes and their religion did not play a major reason for the dropouts. Place of birth, like urban or rural, type of family, marital status (married and unmarried) and employment status were not influenced by the psychological factors as a reason for the dropouts.

3. The following family related factors were reasons for dropouts:

There is a relationship between family-related factors, namely, more time spent on children's care, heavy workload, family expenditure, lack of motivation by family members and scarcity of money, and the following personal attributes—gender, educational qualifications, annual family income, marital status, place of birth and type of family—play a vital role as a reason for the dropouts.

4. The following family related factors were not reasons for dropouts:

There is no relationship between family-related factors and the following personal attributes: age, religion, community and employment status that are non-influential. Family-related factors and the students studying in different universities did not influence as confronting factors for the dropout in the distance education stream.

5. The following social-related factors as reasons for drop-outs:

There is a relationship between social-related factors, namely, too much of family restriction, marriage, religious restriction, and the following personal attributes, age, marital status and type of family of dropouts. The related social factors play a proximate role as a reason for the dropouts in the distance education stream.

6. The following social related factors were not as reasons for dropout:

The place of different university studied does not play a major role in social-related factors as a reason for the dropouts. Indeed gender, educational qualification, religion, community, employment status, place of birth and family's annual income did not play a role in association with the social-related factors as a reason for the dropouts.

7. The following health-related factors were reasons for dropouts

There is a relationship between health-related factors, namely, physical handicap, chronic ill health, children's ill health and elder's ill health, and the personal attributes. The analysis shows that a majority of the dropouts in this category belong to Madras University compared to Madurai Kamaraj University and Bharadhidasan University.

8. The following health-related factors were not reasons for dropouts:

There is no relationship between health-related factors and the following personal attributes: age, gender, religion, community, educational qualification, employment, type of family, marital status, place of birth and family's annual income of the dropouts.

9. The following education related factors were the reasons for dropouts:

Educational-related factors, namely the syllabus reflecting high standard, lack of library facilities, lack of job orientation, lack of comprehension of the subjects, lack of facility to discuss with peer members regarding subject and syllabus were the reasons for the dropouts. It has come to be known that the students belonging to different universities, educational qualifications (undergraduate and postgraduate levels), gender, age group, employment, family's annual income and marital status were the reasons explained by the dropouts. Indeed, these above mentioned are socio-economic reasons given as causes for the dropouts.

10. The following education-related factors were not reasons for dropouts:

There is no relationship between education related factors and the following personal attributes, place of birth, family type, religion and community, and these do not play a major role as a reason for the dropouts.

11. The following employment-related factors were reasons for the dropouts:

There is a relationship between employment-related factors, namely, heavy workload in the office, job and promotional opportunities, transfer to another post/place and new responsibility in the office, and the following personal attributes: age, gender, educational qualifications, employment status, community and family's annual income which play a vital role as reasons for the dropouts.

12. The following employment-related factors were reasons for the dropouts:

There is no relationship between employment-related factors and the following personal attributes: religion, marital status and type of family which do not play a major role as reasons for the dropouts.

13. The following economic-related factors were reasons for the dropouts:

There is a relationship between economic-related factors, namely high tuition fees, unable to bear the tuition and examination fees and non-availability of scholarship, and personal attributes: educational qualification, marital status and family's annual income which play a vital role in association with the economic-related factors as a reason for dropouts.

14. The following economic-related factors were not reasons for the dropouts:

There is a no relationship between economic-related factors and the following personal attributes: age, gender, religion, community, employment, place of birth and type of family as a major reasons for the dropouts.

15. The following institutional-related factors were reasons for the dropouts:

There is a relationship between institutional-related factors, namely, absence or delay in dispatch sending of study materials, inadequate library facilities and high tuition fees and lack of proper public relations, and the following personal attributes: age, educational qualifications, religion, community, employments, family annual income and place of birth which play a vital role in association with institutional-related factors as reasons for the dropouts. Different universities have different institutional factors as reasons for the dropouts.

16. The following institutional related factors were not reasons for the dropouts:

There is no relationship between institutional related factors and the following personal attributes: sex, marital status and type of family which are not influenced by institutional-related factors as reasons for the dropouts.

Discussion

The main objective of the study is to fathom the reasons for dropouts in three universities, namely, Madras University, Madurai Kamaraj University and Bharathidasan University, Trichrappalli. The reasons for the dropouts were analysed in eight different dimensions and with regard to socio-economic background.

The eight different dimensions in which the reasons for dropouts were probed were psychological-related factors, sociological-related factors, family-related factors, educational-related factors, institutional-related factors, employment-related factors, economic-related factors and health-related factors.

The above eight dimensions were taken as an independent variable to probe the reasons for the dropouts. The nature of the study was synchronic in nature in which the data were collected from three different universities to identify the dropouts with the help of validated questionnaire.

The responses of the dropouts were analysed in tables by applying appropriate statistical techniques. The analysis of the table concludes the ameliorative and amendable results. The analysis explicitly shows that there are many axial factors that play a proximate role as reasons for the dropouts.

It comes to light that family-related factors and economic-related factors occupy a concomitant role in the distance education stream as main reasons for the dropouts. Besides the above-mentioned two factors, institutional-related factors, psychological-related factors and occupational-related factors also act as major factors in the continuing distance education stream for the learners.

Indeed, the analysis elucidates the fact that health-related factors and social-related factors influence to a low level as major factors for the dropouts.

The analysis reveals that many of the combating factors gives reasons for the dropouts. Many of the dropouts are of the opinion that the syllabus for the prescribed course comprises watertight subjects that are difficult to understand. A majority of the distance education learners are in the stage of adulthood and hence provision of flexible learning material would help them to improve their retention capacity.

From the interviews with the distance learners, it becomes clear that personal contact programmes have to be organised in different nodal places instead of in the university itself for all the courses.

The distance learners further feel that the majority of the subjects have to be linked to employment opportunities, and their learning and successful completion of the course should be facilitating vertical mobility. But from the heart-to-heart talk with the dropouts of distance education, it is revealed that the university should play a flexible role in enrolling the learners, and help them by providing all possible assistance for the successful completion of the course.

The dropouts feel that the university faculties should be accessible to learners with a friendly paternal attitude, and help them to complete the course without any confrontations.

According to the study, 63.49 per cent of the dropouts in three different universities are willing to continue their studies in the distance education stream but 36.51 per cent expressed their unwillingness to continue their studies due to various domestic and others problems.

A majority of the dropouts expect that the university should have some tie-up with some nationalised banks for providing educational loans to the needy learners. As in the case of the Indira Gandhi National Open University, the other distance education universities may also permit learners to take examinations without collecting separate examination fees.

Term-end examinations can be conducted every Saturday and Sunday instead of conducting them at a stretch. This will help the distance learners to prepare and write the examinations better.

CONCLUSIONS

If the conclusion of this study is taken note of by all the directorates of distance education / universities, there will be a substantial decline in the percentage of dropouts. Offering student-friendly distance education programme will reduce the dropout rate in distance education substantially and help the students to successfully complete their degree / diploma courses of their choice. They will definitely benefit by this mode of education that will eventually lead to suitable employments and career advancements.

Appendix

U.G.C. Major Research Project on "A Study of Dropouts in Distance Education in Tamil Nadu"

Dear Respondent,

University Grants Commission has given me an opportunity to undertake the Major Research Project titled "A Study of Dropouts in Distance Education in Tamil Nadu". In this connection, I am enclosing the stamped envelope along with this questionnaire to enable you to return the same. Please return the filled questionnaire without fail. I assure you that your response will be used only for research purpose and will be kept absolutely confidential.

Seeking your cooperation for the successful completion of this study.

Thanking you,

Yours Sincerely

(V.P. Matheswaran)

University of Madras
Department of Adult and Continuing Education
U.G.C. - Major Research Project on
"A Study of Dropouts in Distance Education in Tamil Nadu"
Questionnaire Schedule

1. Name of the University : 1) Bharathidasan 2) Madras
   3) Madurai Kamaraj
2. Name of the Degree : 1) P.G. or U.G.
   2) Subject: __________
3. Sex : 1) Male 2) Female
4. Age : 1) 18-22 2) 23-27
   3) Above 27
5. Marital Status : 1) Married 2) Unmarried
   3) Widow 4) Divorce
   5) Destitute
6. Religion : 1) Hindu 2) Muslim
   3) Christian 4) Others
7. Community : 1) SC/ ST 2) BC
   3) MBC 4) Others
8. Place of Birth : 1) Rural 2) Urban
9. Type of Family : 1) Nuclear Family
   2) Joint Family
   3) With Parents
10. Annual Family Income : 1) Below Rs.20, 000/-
    2) Rs.20,001/- to Rs.25,000/-
    3) Rs.25,001/- to Rs.30,000/-
    4) Rs.30,001/- and above
11. Parent's Educational Qualifications:
    1) Illiterate 2) Primary
    3) Upper Primary 4) Secondary
    5) Higher Secondary 6) Degree and above
    7) Technical 8) Professional

12. Employment of the Learner:

    1) Employed   2) Unemployed

13. What was the psychological factors responsible for your dropping out?

    1) No intension for further study
    2) Less retention/Memory power
    3) Fear of failure
    4) Inferiority complex
    5) Any other: specify

14. What was the family-related factors responsible for your dropping out?

    1) More time spent on children's care
    2) Heavy workload
    3) Heavy family expenditure\Lack of motivation from family members
    4) Scarcity of money
    5) Any other: specify

15. What was the occupational-related factors responsible for your dropping out?

    1) Heavy workload in the office
    2) Job and promotional opportunity
    3) Transfer from one post to another locally
    4) Transfer to another place
    5) New responsibilities in the office
    6) Any other: specify

16. What was the health-related factors responsible for your dropping out?

    1) Physically handicapped 2) Chronic illness
    3) Children's ill-health   4) Elders' ill health
    5) Any other: specify

17. What are the education-related factors responsible for your dropping out?

    1) Syllabus reflecting high standard

2) No library facilities
3) Lack of comprehension of the subject
4) Lack of job orientation
5) No facility to discuss the subject with peer
6) Difficult examination system
7) Any other: specify

18. What was the institutional-related factors responsible for your dropping out?
    1) Study materials are not sent in time
    2) Study materials are not at all sent
    3) No proper response from the administration during personal enquiry
    4) Improper conduct seminar
    5) Improper public relation of concerned officials
    6) High tuition fees
    7) No proper response to communication
    8) Any other: specify

19. What was the social-related factors responsible for your dropping out?
    1) Too much of family restriction
    2) Marriage
    3) Unwillingness of spouse
    4) Unwillingness of family members
    5) Any other: specify

20. You may rank the following factors that influenced you to drop out:
    1) Psychological-related factor ( )
    2) Family-related factor ( )
    3) Social-related factor ( )
    4) Health-related factor ( )
    5) Educational-related factor ( )
    6) Employment-related factor ( )
    7) Institutional-related factor ( )

Bibliography

Adiseshiah Malcolm S. (1974), "Concern over large number of dropouts in schools". In M.B. Buch (Ed.), *Fourth Survey of Research in Education.* op.cit.

______________ (1990), "Strategies for Distance Education", *Kakatiya Journal of Distance Education,* School of Distance Learning and Continuing Education, Kakatiya University, A.P., July-December, Vol.1, No.2.

Alsagoff (1985), *A Study of Learning Styles,* Student's Characteristics and Faculty Perception of Distance Education Programme at University Sains Malaysia, E.D.D. University of Washington order No DA 8529884 P 280 (Dissertation).

Anderson, H.T. et. al. (1977), "An Exploratory Study of Correspondence Course", Unpublished Manuscript, University of Illinois, CHAPAIGN-Urbana (ERIC Document Reproduction No. Ed 013371).

Antonia, M. Alvarez (1990), "Research into Post Graduate Distance Education", Evaluation of the course on Translation Studies at UNED, Spain.

Anupreet, S. (1999), "Education department clueless on drop-out rate", *Indian Express,* 30, July 1999.

Asha S. Knowles (Ed.): (1988), *The International Encyclopedia of Higher Education: Issues and Prospectus,* WIN of ICDE, Financed by UNICEF, Madras.

Bartels, John (1983), "Study Experience of Graduates and Dropouts at the Fern University", *ICDE Bulletin,* Vol, 7, January.

Bath, J. (1984), "Research on Completion and Discontinuation in Distance Education", *Episttolo Diadaktika, the Journal of Correspondence Education,* European Home Study Council 1&2.

Bombay Municipal Corporation (1956), "The incidence of Dropouts in Primary Schools in work (Electoral ward no 31) for six months between September 1955 and February 1956 and factors responsible for the same ", In M.B. Buch (Ed.), *Second Survey of Research in Education,* Baroda, SERD.

_______________ (1967), "Study of the incidence of wastage and stagnation and effectiveness of our educational efforts", In M.B. Buch (Ed.), *Second Survey of Research in Education,* Baroda: SERD.

Brown, Sewart, D. (1983), "Learning to use Video Replay", *Teaching at a Distance,* No.23, Summer.

Christos, Pierrakees and Michalis Xenos (2004), "A comparative study of dropout rates and causes for two different distance education courses", *International Review of Research in Open and Distance Learning,* Vol.5, No.2, Aug. Greece.

Cochran Sylvia (2009), "Why a high rate of dropout for distance learning students?"www.brighthub.com/education/online-earning/article/33547.aspx.

Crooks (1987), "Open Learning Systems", *Indian Journal of Open Learning,* January, Vol.9. IGNOU, New Delhi.

Das, R.C. (1970), "An investigation into the problem of wastage and stagnation at the primary level of education in the district of Sibasafan", in M.B. Buch (Ed.), op.cit..

Daniel, J. (1984), "The future of Distance Teaching Universities in a World -Wide Perspective", *Courier* No.30 Paper 7 ASBAE.

_______________ (1989), "Commonwealth of Learning Opens", *ICDE Bulletin,* January, Vol.9.

Deshmuk, K.G. (1986), "Genesis and Growth of Distance Education", *University News,* New Delhi, Vol. XXXIV, No.42.

Dickens (1984), *The history of Continuing Education for black people in the Roxbury Community,* 1900-1980, E.D.D. Boston University, Order No.DA9207617 P.224 (Dissertation).

Directory of Distance Education Institutions Part-I. (1991), India, Association of Indian Universities and Common Wealth Learning, New Delhi.

Directory of Distance Education Institutions, Part-II. (1991), Pakistan & Sri Lanka, Association of Indian Universities and Common Wealth Learning, New Delhi.

Donehower, G. (1968), "Variable Associated with Correspondence Study", A Study to Test Twelve Hypothesis (M.A. Thesis), Nevada University.

Dutt, N. et-al. (1982) "Educational Backwardness of Girls in Harayana State", In M.B. Buch (Ed.), *Fourth Survey of Research in Education,* NCERT, New Delhi.

Dutt, Rudder (1983), "Planning and Development of Distance Education in India", Paper presented in Annual meeting of IUACE at Pune University, New Delhi.

Eisenberg et.al. (1990), "Student Dropout from a Distance Education Project Course", A new method of analysis, *Journal of Distance Education,* Vol.II, No.II

Freitas, K.S., et-al. (1986), "Factors affecting student success at the National Open University of Venezuela", *Distance Education,* Vol.7, No.1, March.

Gadgil, D.R. and Dandekar, V.M. (1995) "Report of two Investigations—Primary Education in Satara District" In M. B. Buch (Ed.), *Second Survey of Research in Education,* Baroda: SERD.

Gangoparthyag, S.K. (1985) "Sociological study of the causes of dropouts and repeats in secondary schools", in M.B. Buch (Ed.), *Fourth survey research in education,* op.cit.

Garg, S.C. et-al. (2004), "Open and Distance Learning in India: IGNOU's Contribution to Indian Society", *University News,* 42 (46), Nov.15-21.

Gerard Lassibille and Lucia Navarvo (2007), "Why do higher education students dropouts? Evidence from Spain" *Education Economics,* Vol.16, Issue 1, www.econpapers.repec.org/article/tafedecon/v.

Gladden (1988), *Continuing Education Colleges and Universities: Current role scope of trends,* Ed.D. University of Arkanasas, Order No. DA 8818273, P.173.

Gladieux Lawrence & Laura Perna (2005) *Borrowers who Dropout, A neglected aspect of the college student loan trend,* National Center For Public Policy and Higher Education. www.highereducation.org/reports/borrowing

Gupta (1986-87), "Finances of Higher Education", *Journal of Higher Education,* Vol. 12, Nos. 1-3, U.G.C. New Delhi.

Gupta, M. (1987), "A study of Institute of Correspondence Studies, University of Rajasthan", *Journal of Higher Education,* vol.12, No.1-3.

Gupta, M.P. (1994), "Impact of Distance Education in learners of DDE course in Rajasthan", DDE Project work, IGNOU.

Hakemulder, J. (1978), *UNECADE, Some Thoughts on Distance Education,* Addis Ababa, United Nations (EGA).

Harrington, F. (1979), *The Future of Adult Education,* Londen Jossey-Bass.

Harris, W.J.A. et al. (1977), *A Hand Book of Distance Education,* Manchester Monographs 7, Department of Adult and Higher Education, Manchester, U.K.

Harter, D. (1969), *Why Suny students Fail to Complete Independent Study Course,* State University of New York [NY 1969], [ERICED035814].

Harwood (1985), "Seoul's Super School", *ICDE Bulletin,* Vol.8, May.

History of Higher Education in South India (1957), Vol. I & Vol. II, University of Madras 1857-1957, Madras.

Holmberg, B. (1981), *"Status and Trends of Distance Education",* Kogen Page, London, United Kingdom.

_______________ (1995), Theory and Practice of Distance Education, London, Routledge, UK.

Hommadi, A.H. (1990), *Open University,* Indian Bibliographies Bureau, Delhi.

H.R.D. Report (1999), School Drop-out Rate continues to be alarming: HRD report, *The Hindustan Times,* New Delhi, 3rd May.

Hugh W. Springer [Ed.]: (1993), *The Commonwealth Universities Year Book-1992,* Vol III. The Association of Commonwealth Universities, London.

Indian Express (1993), Madurai Edition: Monday, May 10, p.10.

Inglis, Paul (1987), "Distance Teaching Us Deal, Long Live Distance Learning or Autonomy in Distance Learning", *ICDE, Bulletin,* Vol. 15 September.

Jose, Chander N. (1991), *Management of Distance Education,* Sterling Publishers Pvt. Ltd., New Delhi.

_______________ et. al. (1985), Dropout in Distance Education", A case study of effectiveness of the University Instructional Television Fixed System - Ph.D., Thesis, University of origin.

Jayasankar, K. (1993), "Quality of Distance Education", Presidential Address in first national conference held at Kakatiya University.

Kamat, A.R., Deshmukh, A.G. (1963) "Wastage in college Education", In M.B. Buch (Ed.), *Second Survey of Research in Education,* op.cit.

Keegan, Desmod. J. (1980), "Drop out at the Open University", *Australia Journal of Education,* Vol.21, 1, March.

_______________ (1986) *The Foundation of Distance Education,* St. Martins Press, New York.

Kemer, David (1989), "A Longitudinal process model of drop out from Distance Education", *The Journal of Higher Education,* Vol.60, No.3, May-June, Ohio State University Press.

Kennedy, D, et.al. (1976) "Student Progress and withdrawal", *Teaching at a Distance,* 7, pp. 61-75.

Koul, B.N. et al., (Ed) (1982), *Studies in Distance Education,* Association of Indian Universities and IGNOU, New Delhi.

Kulandaiswamy, V.C. (1992), Distance Education in Indian Context, *Indian journal of Open learning,* Vol.1, No.2.

______________ (2002), Distance Education: The third stage in evolution of education, Zakir Hussain Memorial Lecture held in Gandhigram Rural Institute, Dindigul, December 28.

Latiff, Abdul, (1988), Role conflict, role ambiguity and job satisfaction among faculty members in a distance education system. A case study at the University of Science Malaysia, Ph.D., thesis, Indiana University, Order No. DA8902531, p.240.

Lee, C. Deighton [Ed.]: (1971), *The Encyclopedia of Education,* Vol. 2, The Macmillan Company and the free press, U.S.A.

Mani Gomathi, (1983), "Evaluation of Distance Education", Unpublished Ph.D. thesis, submitted to the University of Madras, Chennai.

______________ (1988), (Ed.) *Women in Distance Education*: Issues & Prospects", WIN of ICDE.

Marshall Jane (2009), Why dropouts drop out" Article in University *World News,* Issue: 77, 24 May www.universityworldnews.com.

Matheswaran, V.P. (1994) "Distance Education through Mother Tongue" *Research Editorial,* Published by Indian Tamil Teachers Association, Vol.I, Pp.1033-38.

______________ (1995) "A study of Attitude of Distance Learners towards Open Learning Systems with special reference to Indira Gandhi National Open University, New Delhi", Ph.D. thesis submitted to the University of Madras.

______________ (1995) "Open Education System and its Reforms" *Research Editorial,* Indian Tamil Teachers Association, Vol.I, pp.947-951.

______________ (1996) "Contribution of Distance Education in Women's Development" Research Editorial, Indian Tamil Teachers Association, Vol.I, pp.1127-1130.

______________ (1998) "Attitudinal study of Open Learners hailing from IGNOU", *Recent Researches in Education and Psychology,* Chandigarh. Vol.3, No.I-II.

______________ (2001), "Utilisation of the Supporting Service Systems by IGNOU learners", *Educational Review,* Bangalore, Vol.44, No. 1.

______________ (2002) "Universities in Promoting Adult Education", *University News,* Association of Indian Universities, Vol.40, No.31, August 05-11.

______________ (2005), *Distance Education: Student Support Services,* Book, Anmol Publication Pvt. Ltd., New Delhi.

Mathur, J.S., Jain, S.P. and Rahim, C.A. (1982), "Rural Youth from poverty groups, Dropouts and non-students, A study of four States", In M.B. Buch (Ed.), *Fourth Survey Research in education.*

McHenry, Robert. (Ed.) (1994), *Britannica Book of the Year 1993,* Encyclopedia Britannica Inc. Chicago.

Medhi, S. (1978), "An Investigation into the probable causes of stagnation and wastage among the pupils of secondary schools". In M.B. Buch (Ed.) *Third Survey of Research in Education,* op.cit..

Menmuir, K. (1982), "Educational Technology by Distance L.arning", *Media in Education and Development,* 14 (4): 9-11.

Mohanty, Jagannath (1992), "Development of Distance Education", *Journal of Planning and Administration,* July, Vol.VI, No.3.

Moonis Raza (Ed.), (1957), *Higher Education in India,* Acharya Book Depot, New Delhi.

Moore, M.G. (1987), "Learners and Learning at a Distance", International Council for Distance Education, *Bulletin,* 14.

Murali (1993), "Selected Case Studies of Women learners who had Dropped out of Open Learning System of the Madras University , M.A., Project work, University of Madras.

Murugan, K. (1994), "The status and prospects of councillors training: The IGNOU Experience", *Indian Journal of Open Learning,* Vol.3, No.1, IGNOU, New Delhi.

Narayanaswamy Vatsala (1983), "Potential Dropouts in Middle Schools Levels", In M.B. Buch (Ed.), *Third Survey of Research in Education.* op.cit.

Nagarajan, K. (1982), *The Annamalai University 1929-1979: A Short History,* Annamalai University, Chidambaram.

National Knowledge Commission Report (2007), Government of India

Oblender, T. E. (2002), A hybrid course model: One solution to the high online drop-out rate. *Learning & Leading with Technology,* 29(6), 42-46.

Parker, A. (1995), Distance Education Attrition, *International Journal of Educational Telecommunications,* 1(4), 389-406.

____________ (1999), A study of variables that predict dropout from distance education. *The International Journal of Educational Technology,* 1(2). Available online at: http://smi.curtin.edu.au/ijet/v1n2/parker (accessed 17 November 2005).

Paulraj (1979), "A study of Socio-Economic factors and their inter-relationships among the out-of-school children", In M.B.Buch (Ed.), *Fourth Survey of Research in Education,* op.cit.

Peters, Otto (1992), "Some observations on dropping out in Distance Education" *Journal of Distance Education,* Vol.13, Isues.2. Routledge, Taylor & Francis Group.

Phythian, E.et.al. (1983), "Dropout from Third Level Maths Courses", *Teaching at a Distance* 23.35-45.

Quinn, Jocey (2004), "Understanding working-class a dropouts from higher education through a socio-cultural lens: cultural narratives and local contexts", *International studies in sociology of education,* Vol.14, Number 1, March, pp.57-74. www.ingentaconnect.com

Ramalinggam, P.V. (1992), "Print materials in distance education: Its importance and need for use of computers for production of good quality print materials, DDE. Project Report submitted to IGNOU, New Delhi.

Rather, A.R. (1985), "Incidence of dropouts and maladjustment among students in relation to creativity and social structure of the school" In M.B.Buch (Ed.), *Fourth Survey of Research in Education,* op.cit.

Rawat, D.S. (1968), "Draft Blue print of Action Plan to reduce wastage and stagnation in the primary and middle schools". In M.B.Buch (Ed.), *Fourth Survey of Research in Education,* op.cit.

Reddy, Eswar V. (1988), *Note of the Open University System with particular reference to correspondence course in the light of UGC policy grants,* Osmania University, Hyderabad.

Reneland Linda (2004), *Learning at a Distance—How to prevent Dropouts,* Vaxjo University, Sweden

Reddy, G. Ram (1987), *Planning Management and Monitoring of Distance Education,* Vol.1, Asia Development Bank, Manila.

Rekkedal, T. (1985), *Introducing the Personal Tutor / Counsellor in the System of Distance Education,* Stabekk, Norway, NKI, Skolen.

_______________ (1986), "The Tutor Councillor in Norway", *Journal of Open Learning,* Vol.1, No, 1. February.

Roberts D. (1984), "Ways and means of Reducing Early Student Dropout Rates", *Distance Education,* 5, 1, Pp.50-71.

Ruggles, R.H., et.al. (1982) *Learning at a Distance and the New Technology,* Vancouva Educational Research Institute of British ,Columbia..

Rumble, G., Harry, K. [Eds.] (1982), *The Distance Teaching Universities,* Croom Helm, London.

_______________ (1986) *The Planning and Management of Distance Education,* Croom Helm, London.

Sapra, C.L. (1967), "Educational Wastage and Stagnation in India", In M.B.Buch (Ed.), *Second Survey of Research in Education,* op.cit

Sathiyanarayana, P. (1992), *Distance Education: What? Why? and How?* IGNOU, Regional Centre, Hyderabad, A.P.

Sevensson, Lars (2002), "Communities of Distance Education", Ph.D. thesis submitted to Gotaborg University, Sweden.

Shatzmann, Isreal. (1984), "Everyman's University Isreal Original Aims, Interim Results and New Projects", *ICDE Bulletin*, Vol.5, May.

Shin, N. and Kim, J. (1999), An exploration of learner progress and drop-out in Korea National Open University. *Distance Education*, 20(1), 81-95.

Shirgopicar, S.G. (1983), "A Study of Wastage in Education of Girls (Standard VII to X) In the high schools in Kothapur corporation area," in M.B. Buch, *Fourth Survey of Research in Education*, op.cit.

Simpson, O. (2000), *Supporting Students in Open and Distance Learning*, London, UK: Kogan Page Ltd.

Singh, Bakshish (1992), "Correspondence and Distance Education in India. An in depth study", Unpublished Research Project Report, IGNOU.

______________ et al. (1994), "Mechanism of Maintenance of Standards in Distance Education", *Kakatiya Journal of Distance Education*, Kakatiya University, A.P. Jan.June Vol.3, No.2.

______________ et al. (1988), *Students Support Services, Studies in Distance Education*, (Ed) B.N. Koul et al., Association of Indian Universities and IGNOU, New Delhi.

Singh Amrik [Ed.]: (1992), *Universities Hand Book*, Association of Indian Universities, AIU House, New Delhi.

Singh, Gopal (1984), "A Socio-Psychological study of high level dropouts". In M.B.Buch (Ed.), *Fourth Survey of Research in Education*, op.cit.

Spady William G. (1970) "Dropouts from higher education: An interdisciplinary review and synthesis *Journal of interchange*, Vol. 1, No.1, April, 1970. www.springerlink.com.

Spencer (1985), *Continuing Education in Rural areas. Delivery system for Distance education*, E.D.D., University of Montana, Order No. DA 8517594 p.182.

Sweet, R. (1983), Student dropout in distance education: an application of Tinto's model, *Distance Education* 7, pp. 201-213.

Tyler-Smith Keith (1994), *New Federal Adult Learning Journal*, England.

Takwala, R. (1988), "Dimensions and Extensions of Distance and Open Educational Systems," *Studies in Distance Education*, Association of Indian Universities and IGNOU, New Delhi.

Treitals, K.S. et al. (1986), "Factors affecting students success at the National Open University of Venezuela," *Distance Education*, March, Vol.7, No.1.

Tinto, V. (1975), "Dropout from Higher Education:" A Theoretical Synthesis of Recent Research, *Review of Educational Research* 45:89-125.

Towards Equality (1978), "Report of the committee on the status of Women in India", In M.B. Buch (Ed.), *Second Survey of Research in education,* op.cit.

Vergidis, D., & Panagiotakopoulos, C. (2002), Student dropout at the Hellenic Open University: Evaluation of the graduate program, "Studies in Education". *International Review of Research in Open and Distance Learning,* 3(2).

Wedemeyer, James, B. (1959), "Completion of University Correspondence Courses by Adults", *Journal of Higher Education,* 30 (2)

Woodly, Alan (2004), "Conceptualising student dropout in Part time distance education: Pathologising the normal", *The journal of Open/ Distance Learning,* Vol.19, Issue 1, Feb.

______________ and Parlett, M. (1983), "Student Drop-out", *Teaching at a Distance,* 24, 2-23.

Wang Jenny (2000), "Strategies for Reducing Dropout from Distance Education courses". www.editlib.org

Xenos, M., Pierrakeas, C., & Pintelas, P. (2002), A survey on student dropout rates and dropout causes concerning the students in the course of informatics of the Hellenic Open University. *Computers & Education,* 39(4), 361-377.

Yukselturk, Earman et.al. (2006), "Examining the factors affecting student dropout in an Online Certificate Programme", *Turkish Online Journal of Distance Education*—TOJDE, July.

Index